SHIRLEY'S STORY

SHIRLEY'S STORY

A tale of strength, courage, and hope

EMILY EKLUND POWER

PEPPER PRESS

First published in 2023 by Pepper Press, a division of Fair Play Publishing
PO Box 4101, Balgowlah Heights, NSW 2093, Australia
www.pepperpress.com.au

ISBN: 978-1-925914-64-1

ISBN: 978-1-925914-65-8 (ePub)

The following is a true story. Dates, events, conversations, and names are based on memories collected by Shirley Singh, and her recollection of them. Some names, identities, and circumstances have been changed to protect the integrity or anonymity of the individuals involved. Some information has been redacted to protect privacy while some information was learned post–legal proceedings. Conversations are not written to represent word-for-word documentation but a recollection of them. Some situations have been compressed, and others told in a way to evoke real feeling and meaning of what was said.

Cover photograph of Shirley Singh by Marigold Meagher, Eve Editorial

All other photographs supplied by Shirley Singh

Cover design and typesetting by Leslie Priestley

All inquiries should be made to the Publisher via hello@fairplaypublishing.com.au

NATIONAL
LIBRARY
OF AUSTRALIA

A catalogue record of this book is available from the National Library of Australia.

To Archana, Neelma, Kunal, and Sidhi.

May the road rise to meet you,

may the wind be always on your back,

may the sunshine fall on your faces,

may God hold you in the hollows of his hands,

until we meet again.

A message from Shirley

Every day I light four candles.

One for each of my children who has departed this earth.

I watch the glow of the light warmly lick the walls; the same walls which once reverberated with my children's laughter and joy.

Even in dysfunction, our family's fierce love for each other could overcome anything.

It still does.

I am proud, so proud, of the beautiful, kind, caring, smart, and funny children we raised.

They were perfect.

I've dedicated my life to my children and I will continue to do so until the day I die.

Every move I make, I see memories of my children.

Every time I close my eyes, I see memories of my children.

That's my reality.

I don't want you to feel sorry for me.

I want you to see strength.

I have survived the worst God can throw at me, four times over.

I'm a fighter, a warrior, and a tiger.

I am forever indebted to the life my children gave me.

And I will forever live life in their honour.

This is our story.

CONTENTS

Prologue   1

Chapter 1: Blood Lines   2

Chapter 2: Orphan   6

Chapter 3: The Early Years   11

Chapter 4: Kidnapped   14

Chapter 5: Our Family   18

Chapter 6: The Flight Home   23

Chapter 7: The Police Station   26

Chapter 8: The Walk-Through   29

Chapter 9: Max   33

Chapter 10: A Career Lady   37

Chapter 11: Relationships Sour   40

Chapter 12: A Bad Husband   43

Chapter 13: Identification   48

Chapter 14: Returning Home   51

Chapter 15: The Funeral   54

Chapter 16: Our Faith   58

Chapter 17: The Affairs   62

Chapter 18: The Showdown   67

Chapter 19: The Emails   70

Chapter 20: My Dreams   73

Chapter 21: Diaries   75

Chapter 22: The Media   78

Chapter 23: The Police   82

Chapter 24: The Support   85

Chapter 25: Losing My Mind   87

Chapter 26: Savouring Memories   91

Chapter 27: The Investigation Heats Up   94

Chapter 28: The Lost Years   97

Chapter 29: The Capture   99

Chapter 30: Time for Justice   102

Chapter 31: Committed to Stand Trial   106

Chapter 32: Cross-Examination   109

Chapter 33: The Police Informer   111

Chapter 34: Footprints   114

Chapter 35: The Impact   118

Chapter 36: The Judgement   133

Chapter 37: Justice   137

Chapter 38: The Hard Yards   140

Chapter 39: Catching a Murderer   143

Chapter 40: A Question of Parole   151

Chapter 41: Together Again   155

Chapter 42: Memories   158

Shirley's Story: The Timeline   161

Endnotes   175

PROLOGUE

Tuesday, April 22, 2003 7:00pm
Suva, Fiji

Startled, I jumped as the phone rang for the third time in as many minutes. I didn't want to answer it. No way. I'd already told the caller to get fucked. Twice.

It had been a tough few months—or should I say years—in the Singh household. Threatening phone calls were common in our family. As were cheating, blackmail, and assault. And that was just the start of it.

Our children's lives had been threatened before, as had mine and that of my husband, Vijay.

But this was different. It felt different.

I knew my children were dead.

CHAPTER 1

BLOOD LINES

OPERATOR: *Police Emergency*
CALLER: *I've got three dead bodies in a bathtub*
OPERATOR: *Do you need an ambulance?*
CALLER: *No, they're underwater*

A phone call made to emergency services from outside our family home in Brisbane, Australia, on April 22, 2003. It was 2:34 pm. Autumn. Blue sky. Maybe 22, 23 degrees.

It was the second call made to emergency services that day. The first, a minute earlier, was cut off.

My husband, Vijay, and I had built our home at Grass Tree Close, Bridgeman Downs—a relatively affluent suburb 16 km north-west of Brisbane city, one year prior.

Our son Kunal chose the block of land.

'It's perfect,' he'd said. 'We can have parties, a tennis court. You can sit with my future children in the gazebo …'

We chose the home's layout from a display package but extended the size of the house to include a rumpus room on the lower level.

We loved entertaining and wanted to make sure we could fit a bar and pool table.

Kunal had been particularly interested in the build, helping us choose everything from the terracotta tiles to the beige paint, our black and gold kitchen bench, and the cooktop. He also drew plans for a pergola and water feature, which we planned to install later.

Homes were large in Bridgeman Downs; brick and mostly double storey.

The suburb was close to schools, churches, retirement villages, and the local cemetery, which was one of the biggest in Brisbane.

We moved into the home on April 11, 2002, with three of our four children: Neelma, Kunal, and Sidhi.

Archana, then 26, lived nearby with her husband, Kavin, an IT hardware accountant whom she'd met at an Indian grocery store six years earlier.

OPERATOR: *How long have you been there, sir?*
CALLER: **Indistinguishable**
OPERATOR: *It's okay, take a deep breath*

The man making the call was Massimo 'Max' Sica.

I remember when I first met Max; it was 1996. Tall, well dressed, and well spoken, he had an air of arrogance about him. He was standing with his wife, Sara, and their two children, Daniel and Brittany, out in front of his parents' house at Trouts Road, Stafford Heights, a working-class suburb about 20 minutes' drive from Brisbane's CBD.

Max and Sara lived in their own house nearby but started visiting regularly.

We had moved into a neighbouring property three years prior, our first home in Australia, after moving from Fiji. We'd considered Melbourne and Sydney but settled on Brisbane as it was green and clean with plenty of new houses. My two brothers lived in Brisbane and it felt like a nice place to call home.

Our home had a double front door in peach paint, and a balcony with ovular cream pillars. The backyard had a pool for the children to keep cool in summer.

Max was the son of Carlo and Anna Maria Sica, Italian immigrants who'd arrived in Australia in 1970, living in New South Wales before moving to Brisbane in 1984. Max had three siblings, Rosanna, Anna, and Claudio. Max was the youngest, born in 1970.

Carlo was an electrician by trade but later opened Naples Pizza Restaurant in Ashgrove, an upmarket inner-city suburb, where many of his family would work. His pizzas were super tasty, and he'd regularly bring them home for his children to enjoy. He was a kind man and popular with all the neighbourhood kids.

Anna Maria Sica, on the other hand, was harder to engage with and a regular grump.

'I hate cleaning, there's always so many children around,' she'd complain,

I enjoyed seeing the kids have fun. Their squeals of laughter were music to my ears; cleaning was the least of my worries.

In the early days we didn't speak to our neighbours much. However, as the years went on, the contact become more frequent. We'd stop for a chat when taking the rubbish out or cleaning the yard.

Carlo also played in a band and they soon started inviting us to his gigs.

At the start, I knew nothing about Max and had no concerns about him. When Sidhi started kindergarten at Stafford Heights in 1996, Max and Sara offered to drive her to school. Their son Daniel was in the same class as Sidhi.

Sara was a pretty lady, with short brunette hair. She was well spoken, friendly, and always had a smile on her face. She would knock on the door to pick Sidhi up and Max would help buckle Sidhi into his two-door grey Honda Prelude. We'd engage in minor chitchat before I'd wave them goodbye.

Then one day in 1997, Max disappeared.

Sidhi later offered an explanation.

'Mum, Aunty Anna's grandson Daniel has no friends at school; no one talks to him. They say his dad is in prison,' she said.

I never asked Anna Maria, or Sara, where Max was. While I was curious, it was rude to pry in another's affairs. Besides, I figured it would be pretty tough without a husband and father around.

'Make sure you look after him, Sidhi... that's what we Singhs do,' I coached her.

Soon after, we found out the truth.

On May 27, 1993, when he was 23 years old, Max was sentenced to nine years imprisonment for 83 offences. He was part of a gang that burned down a police station and attempted to burn down another. He was also done for wilful damage, breaking and entering, stealing, unlawful possession of a firearm, and unlawful use of a motor vehicle.

The judge described the acts as, '... a display of lawlessness on a grand scale.'

Assessed during sentencing by a prison psychologist, it was noted Max had 'significant personality problems and significant signs of psychopathy.'[1] According to the report, 'This man quite clearly produces most of the symptomatology of a borderline personality disorder, mixed with some features of Italian family loyalty.'

He was released on parole in 1996 after serving only three years. On

October 15, 1997, Max threw a Molotov cocktail at a flat in inner-city West End and was returned to prison.[2] It was this same man that called police to report the deaths of my children on April 22, 2003, 'three dead bodies in a bathtub.'

CHAPTER 2

ORPHAN
1961: Suva, Fiji

I sat in the front row of my Year 5 classroom at Vatuwaqa Government Girls School in Suva, Fiji, staring at the blackboard.

Scrawled across it, in big block letters, was the word *ORPHAN*.

In front of me, a 20-something student teacher paced back and forth, deciding on her next victim in today's spelling lesson.

'Shirley,' she announced, gesturing with her hand for me to stand up.

I loved hanging out with my friends at school, but my preferred class was 'play' and my preferred location was far away from the school yard, standing on the roof of my family's double-storey home in Suva, Fiji, flying my kite. I was a cheeky girl, always talking, always mucking around. Spelling lessons certainly weren't top of my agenda.

'Do you know what orphan means?' the teacher queried the class, positioning me at the front of the room for everyone to see.

Along with the rest of my peers, I shook my head.

'Shirley is an orphan,' she announced, quite matter of fact. 'An orphan is someone that doesn't have any parents, whose mother and father are dead.'

I stared at her intently, processing her words. They definitely didn't make any sense.

I knew my father, Ram Dutta, had passed away. I'd watched him get carried away in a coffin when I was five years old. But my mother, Gayatri Dutta? She was at home. Probably washing or cooking or cleaning.

How dare this silly teacher say such a thing!

Angered by her statement, I picked up the blackboard chalk duster and threw it.

As it spiralled end over end towards her head, I hightailed it out of there. Out the door, through the school gates, and down the street.

I ran toward my three-bedroom home that I shared with my mother and my six brothers and sisters in Flagstaff, an upmarket suburb of Suva, around 4 kilometres from the city centre.

* * *

Our home sat high on the hill, its concrete foundation topped by a silver corrugated iron roof and its front garden overflowing with an assortment of colourful roses. Mango, grapefruit, and coconut trees, along with a vegetable patch with taro leaf, cabbage, tomatoes, carrots, eggplant, and cucumber, filled the rest of the yard.

My father had built the concrete home for us after a hurricane on January 28, 1952, flattened most of Suva, killing more than 20 people and injuring countless more. The winds ripped the roof right off my parents' timber home; almost everything was destroyed. Apparently the winds in Suva were clocked at more than 240 km per hour—before the meteorological department's anemometer was blown away.[3]

Our home was one of the first concrete homes to be built in the area. A decade later, there were concrete homes everywhere.

I shared a large room and a bed with my mum while two of my brothers shared a fancy iron bed with a brass backboard in the same room. I moved into mum's bed after I outgrew my cot and my father passed away.

Back in those days, it was very common for families to share rooms and beds. I actually have no idea how anyone *made* any babies with so many children around!

One of the windows had a beautiful view of our gardens, as well as the streets and shops of Flagstaff.

Like the rest of the house, the front stairs—around 20 of them—were concrete. I'll never forget those stairs! If I ever wanted to go to the movies, mum would give me chores which usually included scrubbing the footpath and stairs with a bucket of water and raking the backyard. Even though my brothers were more interested in playing soccer than going to the movies, they would always help me complete my tasks.

* * *

'Ma, Ma!' I squealed, skidding through the front steps of our house in Vesi Street.

I ran up the stairs, taking two at a time, and down the timber hallway, throwing open doors to my left and right as I moved.

'Maaaaaaaa!!'

And there, like always, in a timber outhouse that had somehow survived the hurricane of 1952, was my mother. Stooped over a tin bucket and board, scrubbing the family clothes.

'Munia!' mum squealed, using my pet name. 'What are you doing home?'

'My teacher told me you were dead … that I was an orphan!' I spluttered, grabbing at her arms and cheeks as I spoke. 'But you're not, you're still alive! You must come to my school to show them!' I insisted, snatching her hand in a tight grip and dragging her towards the door.

She stopped suddenly, pulling me towards her.

'They are lying, Shirley, don't listen to them,' she said. 'You hear me, they don't know what they are talking about.'

'You have to tell them, Mama, you have to tell them you're alive!'

Upon our arrival at the school, the principal, Mrs Deoki, looked concerned. She apologised profusely for the error.

I was very relieved Ma was alive and the school was sorry for their mistake.

However, it would be another five years before I realised the true meaning behind that day.

It was day one of high school, 1966; I was 15 years old.

I'd sat my entrance exam—a prerequisite for Fijian high schools at the time—and enrolled in my subjects, including my favourites of history, biology, and geography.

The principal, Mr Shah, started calling students' names, in order for them to collect their enrolment papers and head to their first class.

I stood, waiting for my name.

'Shirley Dutta, father's name Shiri Kissun Maharaj,' he called, glancing up from the clipboard as he spoke.

'Shirley Dutta, father's name Shiri Kissun Maharaj,' he repeated.

The group of students dwindled in size, as students collected their materials and walked off.

Eventually, I was the only one left.

'Shirley Dutta?' he asked.

I was hesitant but nodded approvingly.

'Yes … however, my father's name is Ram Dutta, not Shiri Kissun,' I explained, pointedly.

Confused, the principal took me to the office, where he said he would call my primary school for information.

'Okay, okay, I get it,' I could hear him saying. 'I'll speak with her mother.'

Later that night, in a conversation with my mother, I queried her. 'Why are people saying my pitaji is not my pitaji?' I asked, referencing the name for one's father in Hindi, my native language. 'Why are they saying Shiri Kissun Maharaj is my father?'

From there, my world unravelled.

My adopted 'mother,' Gayatri Dutta—sitting in front of me—was actually my aunty, and my adopted 'father,' Ram Dutta, was actually my uncle, my mother explained.

I had two half-sisters and five half-brothers from my biological mother's and father's first marriages.

My birth mother, Karam Pati, had died from blood poisoning six days after my birth at the Colonial War Memorial Hospital in Suva, and my biological father—Shiri Kissun Maharaj, a farmer—was unable to look after me.

Given the circumstances, a decision was made by my uncles and aunties to adopt me, and my chosen parents were my mataji (the Hindi word for mother), Gayatri Dutta, and my pitaji, Ram Dutta.

I was the youngest of seven in the Dutta family, and from very early on, my brothers and sisters—Virendra, Trishulla, Ashok, Girlie, Jayant, and Bhagwan (nicknamed Turbert by the family)—loved me as their own.

Virendra was like a father figure. The oldest of my siblings, he worked two jobs to look after us. He was very handsome, with shiny black hair. He was such a hardworking man and so respected by my younger brothers. We were devastated when he passed away on October 29, 1995.

My sister Trishulla treated me like her little baby; she cared for me so much. However, when I was three or four she married and moved to the western side of Fiji, about 140 km away, and I didn't see her often.

My second oldest brother, Ashok, was popular, good-looking, and smart. He once sat a maths test and scored the highest mark in the colony. He was also very loving and caring. He would give me shoulder rides while running up the hill to our house; I would grab onto his hair so I didn't fall off. He also taught me how to dance to rock'n'roll. He sadly passed away on January 28, 2018, at his home in Vancouver, Canada.

Girlie kept to herself a lot but was very close to mum. She was a cleanaholic who constantly wiped the windows and polished the floor. One time, Virendra slipped and fell because the floor was so polished; he was very mad! Like all my brothers and sisters, Girlie always looked after me.

Jayant was nicknamed Lala by the family. He was kind and gentle. When we went out mum would tie my hair tightly in two plaits with the ends sticking up, like Pippi Longstocking. 'Don't do it that tight, it's hurting her,' he'd say, loosening the plaits and combing my hair.

Turbert and I were only a few years apart and would play together often. He was just like our pitaji, and always looking out for me.

Dad treated us girls like angels. To him, we shouldn't be washing clothes, scrubbing floors, or cooking. Turbert and Jayant felt the same way.

Turbert made my first kite out of bamboo, which he later taught me how to fly. He also taught me how to play marbles, which we would enjoy for hours in the backyard. Turbert always won.

I was so lucky to be welcomed by the Duttas. They treated me like a princess and one of their own. I felt angry when people said I was adopted, because in my eyes, I was meant to be in the Dutta family. My dynasty was Maharaj but my family name—and my heart—was with the Duttas. To this day, I still sign my name as Shirley Dutta.

Family was—and still is—the most important thing to me.

The ones who were there when no one else was. That was family.

CHAPTER 3

THE EARLY YEARS

My father Ram had been a kind man, well respected in the community and one of only two Indian men to work at the government's Treasury department. When my biological mother died and my biological father wasn't in a position to look after me, it was Ram who made the decision to adopt me. He named me after two of his favourite actresses, Shirley Temple and Shirley MacLaine, which was uncommon for that time as Indians rarely had English names. He sought to provide me with the best upbringing possible.

My mother and Ram married when my mother was nine and Ram was eleven. Of course, that was the Indian custom back then; you definitely wouldn't see people marrying that young these days.

One of my earliest memories of Ram was of him purchasing fabric from the haberdashery store in the city and asking Ma to make me a dress. It was yellow with red and green flowers and two or three layers of frills. I twirled around the house in it for hours.

On most nights, Ram would return home from work with gifts for me and my siblings. Small packets of unshelled peanuts from Suva's city bus stand were among his favourites. He'd lift me up on the kitchen table to sit with him and we'd remove the roasted peanuts from the small white paper bags before rubbing them between our hands to deshell them. They were super crispy and so tasty.

He would then shower, pour himself a scotch, and sit down for dinner.

When I was five and a half, my pitaji fell ill from alcohol poisoning. Soon after, he died. To me he never looked drunk, but his drinking had ultimately led to his premature death at the age of 42.

I remember seeing him in the coffin at his funeral and being confused by what had happened.

'Why is he sleeping? Why can't we get him back out of the box?' I questioned. Later I wondered why he wasn't coming home. For years, I would stand on the balcony, waiting for him to drive up the street in his little Mini Minor. But he never did.

My mother never remarried.

* * *

Growing up in 1950s and 1960s Fiji was idyllic. The city itself was quite small. There was a market, post office, library, bus station, school, a few large government buildings, and the Grand Pacific Hotel.

There are 14 provinces, 195 districts, and more than 1,100 villages in Fiji.[4] However, we rarely travelled outside the 'Big Island' of Viti Levu, where Suva is located. Our big trips were always between Suva and Nadi, which could take up to eight hours by bus on a winding, gravel road.

Those that didn't work in the city would spend their days climbing trees for fresh coconuts, fishing, or working in their garden or farms.

My mother's father, Ram Harash Maharaj, was one of my first ancestors to arrive in Fiji. He arrived on the Leonidas, a labour transport ship that departed Calcutta, India, on March 3, 1879, and arrived at Levuka, Fiji, on May 14.[5]

Under British colonial rule, Ram Harash was the first of more than 60,000 indentured labourers who would travel to Fiji from India over the next 37 years.[6]

Ram had large sugar cane and rice plantations in Wainibokasi, Nausori, an hour and a half on the gravel road from Suva.

Later, he started a chariot company, moving people by horse and carriage from Wainibokasi to Suva and the Nausori market to get their fresh produce. Later came the establishment of Nausori's first ferry company, followed by a truck and bus company.

My mother's brother, Shree Dhar Maharaj, was also a successful businessman. Shree was born on November 11, 1918—Armistice Day—in Wainibokasi.

When Ram died, Shree was left with the responsibility of providing for his mother and eight siblings, a task that would help mould him as a pioneer, successful businessman, religious leader, and confidant of a prime minister. In 1937, Shree converted a six-cylinder Chevrolet Coupe into a seven-seater bus and operated a service between Nausori and Suva.

He later became the proprietor of Pacific Transport Limited, the largest bus fleet operator in Fiji, and founded Shreedhar Motors Limited. He was the founding president of the Shree Sanatan Dharam Pratinidhi Sabha of Fiji, a cohesive Hindu religious organisation that promotes education to children of all races in Fiji. He also built a secondary school on ten acres of land at Wainibokasi. To date, Pacific Transport is still one of the largest bus manufacturers and transport companies in Fiji with offices in Suva, Sigatoka, Nadi, Lautoka and Taveuni.

Despite being raised by a single mum with seven children, my siblings and I were never short of a penny—mainly thanks to Virendra's work as a cab driver and at the Royal New Zealand Air Force. He always helped support the family.

Sundays were one of my favourite days of the week. That's when mum would take us to the beach at Suva Point, not far from our house. She'd stock a bamboo basket with boiled tapioca, sardines, and tomatoes and we'd spend our time swimming, playing in the sand, and eating.

Tapioca was very popular in Fiji. Like potatoes, you would peel and boil it in salt. It was very starchy. In fact, people would often use leftover tapioca water to starch their clothes.

Sardines were my favourite. I particularly loved eating them with dahl and rice.

Mum travelled to the Suva Municipal Market once a fortnight to get additional fresh green vegetables and root products like taro and cassava, as well as seafood. Back then, you could get eight or nine freshwater crabs for maybe $2 AUD. She would pack her purchases into cotton bags and I'd meet her at the bus stop to help carry the shopping back to the house.

We'd collect eggs from a coop built by Virendra and Ashok at the rear of our property, fry them with ghee, and eat them with bread; they were my absolute favourite and two was never enough.

Food, and the enjoyment of a meal together, was very sacred to our family and our culture. The importance of sharing a meal at the family table was something our parents instilled in us, and something I'd continue with my own children years later.

CHAPTER 4

KIDNAPPED
October 1970

I was 19 years old when I was kidnapped. It was the first of many significant events that would shape my life over the next fifty years.

His name was Maan Singh.

Maan was handsome and friendly but rough around the edges. He was a mechanic, chain smoker, and heavy drinker who was helping raise his five siblings after the death of his father.

As I stood swaying to a performance by my cousin Roshni at an Independence Day festival in Fiji, Maan appeared. To the warm sounds of tabla and sitar, and a kaleidoscope of traditional dancers, I followed Maan outside.

Mum wasn't a fan of Maan. 'He's low grade, not good enough for you, Shirley,' she'd say.

However, here I was, propelled by both fear and intrigue, following him to his car.

'We'll just talk for a bit,' he explained. He smelled of beer and cigarettes, which he puffed on constantly.

The night was warm, the humidity high.

As we climbed into his car—which he'd borrowed from a client—the sound of the music dimmed. I became very aware of just how far away my friends and family were.

Suddenly, he took off, dust rising from the road in our wake.

It was the last time I'd see my family for six months.

* * *

Twelve weeks later, I was married; an Indian wedding ceremony at Maan's mother's house in Kinoya, a housing authority area maybe 30 minutes from the city by car.

Around 70 to 80 of Maan's family and friends attended. But none of mine.

I missed my mother and my brothers. I was distressed.

Mum thought I'd left on purpose; that I'd rebelled against their wishes. She said I'd disgraced them.

A few weeks later, she sent my cousin Gyan to find me and bring me home.

But with Maan's mother hovering over me, I was forced to say I was happy and in love.

Not long after, Maan's physical abuse started.

The punches, the kicking. He even burned my arms with cigarettes. He also forced me to drink beer, which I'd never had before.

Despite this, we would sleep together often. He was a good-looking man who wanted to be fulfilled regularly.

We welcomed our first son, Janel Bahadur Singh, on September 21, 1971.

And ten months later we welcomed a daughter, Janice Suneeta Singh.

They were both easy kids, so sweet and cute.

It wasn't difficult being a first-time mum; I'd learned so much from my own mum in raising kids. However, being separated from my own mother, I was distraught.

I'd sometimes catch the bus to mum's house where she'd look at me with both love and disdain.

'This is what you wanted,' she'd say. 'You chose this life.'

My mum had always given me so much love. I knew I'd hurt her; I knew I'd hurt my family.

After one of Maan's regular beatings, I was forced to flee the house with only the clothes on my back and Janel wrapped in a blanket.

I ran from the home to a local general store, crying and bruised.

This is where my future husband, and father to our four children—Vijay Singh—would see me for the first time.

One of his distant cousins owned the shop and he had just got off at a bus stop nearby.

According to Vijay, 'She was crying in the shop. She looked at me, and our eyes met. She was a little bit cross-eyed and oh, so pretty. I fell for her straight away. There was just something about her. I returned to the shop a few more times with hopes of running into her but it wasn't to be. Lucky for me it would not be long before our paths would cross again.'

I first met Vijay in late 1973 when I started working for Reddy Construction in Moala Street, Samabula, as a receptionist. It was my first job and I would answer the phones and type letters for my manager. Vijay rode the same bus I did home from work, a green Tui Davuilevu 60-seater, which travelled from Suva city to Nausori.

Every time I got on the bus, the only spare seat was always beside him. He later told me this was intentional; he'd keep the seat especially for me.

Vijay was a quiet man but we'd often talk about our families and work. He was one of four children, the son of a womanising dad and a housewife mother. In fact, his own father died of a heart attack while rooting a woman. Fancy that.

Later, when Vijay would piss me off, I would use this info to remind him of his heritage.

Vijay shared how he'd been forced into marriage and wasn't in love with his wife, Sitla. He had one child, with another on the way.

By Vijay's own admission, he was young and naive when his father arranged for him to marry Sitla in January 1972, at 19 years of age. He was six months out of school and working in his first job at Coral Island Motors.

They didn't have much in common—he a city man, she a village girl—and it didn't take them long to realise they weren't happy together.

He felt stuck.

At the same time, I would tell Vijay about Maan, how he beat me and how I wasn't in love with him.

Soon after, Vijay started inviting me to the movies. He would purchase the tickets and reserve the seats but I would never go. Why would I? I had a husband, and he had a wife ... and we both had families.

One day I asked him why he didn't take his wife out.

'I do,' was his response. 'I take her out too.'

I later heard from work friends that they'd seen Vijay at the movies, alone and sobbing. Feeling pained that I had upset him, I finally took him up on the offer to go to a movie. I knew it wasn't the right thing to do but I didn't think anything would come of it.

We went to see the Indian film 'Kati Patang', about a runaway bride who promises her dying widowed friend she will assume her identity and look after her child.

Vijay bought us Twisties and a Coke to share and we sat at the very back of the cinema.

As the movie played, he continued to talk. 'I don't know what to do, I need to leave her, Shirley; I don't want to be with her anymore.'

'Shhh!' I protested, trying to watch the movie.

Then, he tried to kiss me.

While I knew it wasn't the right thing to do, I couldn't help myself … and it wasn't long before I kissed him back.

In the early days, Vijay and I had great chemistry and passion. We'd go to the beach at Vatuwaqa with our woven mat, food, juice, water, and roti curry. Sometimes we'd get passionate in the mangroves behind the beach. Vijay couldn't keep his hands off me; it made me feel so loved and wanted.

Did I feel guilty about my relationship with Vijay? Of course. Sometimes, I'd tell him to go back to his wife. I felt terrible for her. At the same time, I didn't want him to leave me.

CHAPTER 5

OUR FAMILY

Over the next six months Vijay continued to move between my house and that of his wife, Sitla. Eventually though, he stopped going back to her altogether.

Vijay's daughter Nalini, then 18 months old, remained with Sitla, and his second daughter, Kamini, was born in October 1975.

At the start of our relationship, Vijay's children would regularly visit. However, with time, these visits considerably slowed.

Maan also stopped me from seeing Janel and Janice. Because I had cheated, he said I wasn't worthy of looking after the children.

It broke my heart but I felt I wasn't left with any options. I was scared of Maan.

When my son Janel once visited me, he was beaten by his father. Sometimes Maan's sister-in-law Nani would secretly bring the children to me. I'd wrap them tightly in my arms and smother them with kisses; I never wanted them to leave. Later, I'd cry myself to sleep thinking of them.

In spite of the pain we felt being isolated from our children, Vijay and I had a strong relationship filled with a lot of good times. Particularly in the early days. We'd go on picnics and to restaurants, we'd watch movies and party with friends.

We travelled regularly with his brother Ravendra and Ravendra's then-wife, Zubeda, staying at beach resorts in Pacific Harbour with their two children.

In 1975 we made the decision to try for our own family, and across the next 16 years we welcomed four beautiful children to the world: Archana, Neelma, Kunal, and Sidhi.

Archana was our first. Born December 10, 1976, she had a full head of black curly hair and was a very happy baby. When she was little, I would shower each morning and wait to greet the sunrise with her. In Hindu, we believe when the sun rises it gives you life, removes your worries, and leads you to prosperity.

As she grew older, she earned many nicknames, Adu, Archie, and Sonia, which was adopted by her high school friends at Corpus Christi College when they couldn't pronounce her name.

Almost two years later, on December 29, 1978, our second daughter, Neelma, was born. She didn't want to come out; she was ten days late.

Neelma had the most beautiful smile, just like my mum. She had a soft face, naive and innocent. However, she was quick-witted and feisty. She quickly became mummy's little girl. I often called her 'Nim.'

In September 1979, following the births of Archana and Neelma, Vijay started his own company, Unique Motor Spares Limited, with Amrit Patel—a fellow businessman in the motor spare parts industry.

Amrit was such a gentleman and I had a great respect for him. They formed a great partnership and would go on to become one of the best spare parts businesses in Fiji.

Later, we also bought a jewellery shop, Safari Jewellers, on Thompson Street in Suva with my brother-in-law Hari, his accountant wife, Nitya, and their daughter Arti. The shop was filled with gold bracelets, bangles, earrings, and rings. We also sold gifts like wine goblets, ornaments, and clocks. I loved working in that shop.

When Vijay one day heard his younger brother Jaswant was in a relationship with his estranged wife, Sitla, he wasn't angered. In fact, he was happy. It meant he was able to divorce Sitla, leading the way for us to marry.

Vijay and I were married on March 20, 1981, in Suva city, followed by an Indian ceremony with around 20 people at our unit. We ate puri, jackfruit, and split pea curries while overlooking our banana trees decorated with tropical flowers and listening to Indian music.

I wore a red sari covered in gold sequins, and my hair was twisted into a bun. It was a great day, filled with love—we were so excited to officially start our lives together.

A month later, in celebration of my thirtieth birthday, Vijay purchased our first family home in Salato Road, Namadi Heights. It was a beautiful three-bedroom split-level home that I'd desperately wanted but didn't think we could afford. It had decorative timber cornices and a huge lounge and terrace that overlooked the water, a liquor bar, and a large kitchen with an orange tiled benchtop. It was strongly built, and prestigious.

One of my cousins, Vinesh Maharaj, had built the house but ended up selling after he scored residency in the United States.

I had always wanted a house on the hilltop where I could see people, but people couldn't see me. I designed a concrete and wire fence for the yard and planted hibiscus plants, xenias, zebras, and eleven different colours of miniature roses, which we'd use for prayer time.

We loved that home; it was the perfect place to raise kids.

On August 4, 1984, we welcomed our third child, Kunal.

Kunal was born exactly nine months after I completed a holy purification—Shiv Puran Puja—for Lord Shiva. I had only just become a strong devotee of Lord Shiva, and to me, Kunal was a gift from God.

Vijay was so excited to have his first boy and from a young age, he and Kunal would form a lifelong appreciation for cars. Kunal also loved cartoons; his favourite was 'Popeye the Sailor Man.' He was a funny and kind boy, always cheeky and always testing us.

On March 4, 1991, our daughter Sidhi was born. Just like Neelma, she was around ten days late.

Sidhi was absolutely beautiful, witty and cheeky. She said her first word at three months—the Hindi version of grandfather—and started walking when she was only ten months old. She was a very playful little girl and always full of energy.

We adored our children together; they were everything to us.

We also loved the life we had built in Fiji.

However, an uncertain political environment and economy would soon force us west, with Nalini, Kamini, Janel, and Janice also moving to Australia with Sitla and Maan and their respective partners.

We left Fiji for Brisbane on October 31, 1993. It was just over a year after Lieutenant Colonel Rabuka[7] was democratically elected as the country's third prime minister.

Six years prior, on May 14, 1987, Rabuka had staged the first of two military coups to reassert ethnic-Fijian supremacy in Fiji. Alongside soldiers in gas masks and combat gear, he marched into the House of Representatives at gunpoint and asked the 28 members of Timoci Bavadra's elected government to move outside.[8]

At the time, 46 percent of the Fijian population was Indigenous, while 49 percent was Indo-Fijian.[9] Our political power was growing, and the Fijians didn't like it.

Shops were forced to close and buses and taxis stopped operating. Indian women were gang-raped by Fijian soldiers, their husbands beaten on their way home from work and villagers forced to bathe in raw sewage. Shops were gutted by petrol bombs or attacked in smash and grab raids.[10]

Up to 1,000 Indians a day swarmed the Australian and New Zealand high commissions seeking visas.

I had been born and raised with Fijians; the Islanders are some of the friendliest people on the face of this earth. However, many of them had been forced into this bad behaviour.

Indians feared leaving their homes, sending the kids to school, or opening their shops. Each day, rumours of more attacks would sweep the city.

Indians were emigrating by the dozens, shops had declining sales, and tourism operators had high vacancy and cancellation. Newspaper and printing staff were removed from their offices by armed military and the buildings occupied by soldiers. *The Fiji Times and Fiji Sun* did not go to print for five days.

You can now read about the events of the last six days, following Lt Col Rabuka's bloodless coup d'etat last Thursday, May 14. We reported that the next day. Then came an order from Lt Col Rabuka's Council of Ministers that newspapers in Fiji were prohibited from publishing until further notice. To enforce that point, newspaper and printing staff were removed from their offices by armed military. The buildings were then occupied and surrounded by armed soldiers for several days. Some discussions took place regarding censorship guidelines for newspapers—but were unacceptable for their nature and implementation by both The Fiji Times and the Fiji Sun. So, you were literally kept in the dark. We believe the move by the council to ban newspapers and heavily censor radio was ill conceived and not thought through. It is extremely dangerous to keep people in ignorance, particularly when they know momentous events are going on around them. The news blackout worried people. Rumours were flying left right and centre and leaflet campaigns proliferated. Now we plan to give you the news as it happened; without embellishment or emotion. The Governor General, Ratu Sir Penaia Ganilau and Lt Col Rabuka have assured newspapers the freedom to publish. We hope for our readers' sake it continues.

—**The Fiji Times, 21 May 1985**

On September 25, 1987, Rabuka led a second coup.[11]

He subsequently suspended the constitution, dissolved the parliament, and declared Fiji a republic. The Governor-General, Ratu Sir Penaia Ganilau, was appointed president of the republic, and former Prime Minister Kamisese Mara was reappointed prime minister.

Full civilian rule returned in January 1990 when Rabuka gave up his position as Minister of Home Affairs and returned to barracks as head of the armed forces. The new constitution, drafted in 1990, which guaranteed Indigenous Fijian supremacy, was widely regarded as racist, and even drew comparisons to South Africa's apartheid system.

For Vijay and me, there was no security and no future in Fiji. There was a feeling of instability and danger as Indigenous Fijians gained ascendancy and dominance.

Some of the country's best people—doctors, dentists, professors, and teachers—decided there was no future for them or their families in Fiji and they packed up and left for countries like New Zealand, Australia, the US, and Canada.

It was all very, very sad. The country we loved and the country we had wanted to raise our children in was completely broken.

Rabuka was democratically elected as the country's third prime minister on June 2, 1992. At around the same time we were contacted by the Australian Government. We had previously applied for a Permanent Residency Visa and our entry period to Australia was due to expire.

'The time is right,' Vijay said. 'It's time to start our new life in another country.'

I could not have agreed more. We wanted to provide our children with a good education, a safe home, and a great future. Fiji was not the place for that anymore. Australia would be our new home.

We could not wait to make new memories there.

CHAPTER 6

THE FLIGHT HOME

10 Years Later
Wednesday, April 23, 2003
Air Pacific Flight—Fiji to Sydney,
Sydney to Brisbane

Pins and needles shot through my hands and my heart weighed heavily in my chest.

My eyes were weary; they ached. My lips were parched; they stung.

The same words kept echoing in my head: 'Shirley, it's your children. They've been shot dead.'

I tilted my head back, drawing a breath as I moved. I soon exhaled, pressing my forehead on the window of the Air Pacific plane.

So dark; can't see anything.

'It won't be long, Mrs Singh, we'll have you off the aircraft soon,' an attendant said, noticing my discomfort. We were en route from Nadi International Airport in Fiji to Brisbane, via Sydney.

We had travelled to Fiji for a wedding.

But only hours earlier, I'd taken a phone call from a stranger in Fiji.

The caller, a woman with a thick Indian accent, had called twice to say the same thing.

A young man from Vijay's motor vehicle spare parts business soon repeated her calls.

The Australian evening news was reporting on a triple murder at a house in the suburb of Bridgeman Downs.

It looked like our home, they said.

Within hours, and despite no confirmation from Fiji or Australian authorities, our family had helped us pack our things and we were flying home.

The plane landed, and around us, passengers bustled happily, pulling luggage from overhead lockers and preparing to disembark.

It felt like the world was swirling at speed around me.

It was a flight Vijay and I had taken many times before, both as a couple and with our children. As a family of six, we had made the first of those flights in October 1993 when we moved to Australia.

We'd rented out our Fiji home, shipped our cane furniture, and packed our clothes along with sheets, utensils, and a baby cot we'd custom designed for Kunal. Vijay also sold his shares in Unique Motor Parts to my brother Virendra.

In addition to our home at Stafford Heights, we purchased two investment units in Rydges South Bank and a property in the northern suburb of Zillmere.

On the weekends we'd go to the park or beach, or visit a theme park on Queensland's Gold Coast.

Sea World was one of our favourites. We'd spend our days wearing the kids out at the shops, or on the sand. Then Vijay and I would spend our nights enjoying the nightlife of the Gold Coast, and at its casino.

I loved playing the Money Wheel while Vijay spent his time on the roulette table.

They really were some great times.

* * *

As the seats on the plane emptied, and the aisles cleared, staff began to move around us, cleaning.

I closed my eyes. I heard my children laughing. I loved that.

Beside me, Vijay was silent, eyes closed. I tapped his hand; he flinched.

Ahead of us, three men climbed the stairs of the plane. They walked towards us.

Black suits, white business shirts, dark ties.

The first, a solid Caucasian, with a strong Australian accent, spoke first.

'Mr and Mrs Singh, I'm Detective Senior Sergeant Bryan Paton from the Child Protection and Investigation Unit at Petrie Police Station. This is Detective Sergeant Joe Zitny and this is Arveen Singh, a detective and community liaison officer from Boondall Police Station,' he said, gesturing towards another officer—

Indian, maybe six feet.

Detective Senior Sergeant Bryan Paton removed his badge from his pocket, placing it in front of me.

I nodded as he spoke but heard little of what they said.

It was all too much to bear; too much to take in.

They led Vijay and me from the plane, the last to exit. I was placed in a wheelchair and pushed across the tarmac, the bitumen rolling endlessly underneath me as we moved towards the terminals.

'Mr Zitny, do you know what happened to my children. Are they OK?' I pleaded. 'Please tell me what's wrong, why you're here.'

'We'll let you know soon, Mrs Singh,' he said.

As our bags were carried from the airport carousel towards the exit signs, I remembered I owed Kunal a gift.

'I have to get DKNY!' I exclaimed, gesturing towards the duty-free. 'For Kunal...I promised him.'

I took turns buying the children presents from duty-free on each return trip to Australia. The younger girls usually wanted perfume: Neelma, Dior J'adore; and Sidhi, Elizabeth Arden Red Door. Archana always wanted more traditional stuff from Fiji; frozen or cooked vegetables or clothes.

This time was Kunal's turn.

The officers obliged and I was taken to duty-free where I chose him a DKNY perfume and moisturiser.

As we exited the airport, we were told we would be taken to Petrie Police Station, maybe 30 minutes from the airport.

My body slumped against the inside of the police car door, as I buckled myself in.

'Can we go home?' I questioned.

'Soon,' Joe said.

It was my first time in a police car.

CHAPTER 7

THE POLICE STATION

When we arrived at the Petrie Police Station, Vijay and I were placed in separate interrogation rooms. We were advised something had happened at our house but the police wouldn't tell us what.

I pleaded to return home, to see my children, but I was told it was important I provide them with as much information as possible.

They asked me why we'd gone to Fiji and about my love for our children, the state of our marriage, and our finances. They wanted to know about Vijay's business, any enemies we may have, and the last time I'd spoken to Neelma, Kunal, and Sidhi.

We went to Fiji on April 13, 2003, for the wedding of one of Vijay's staff, Artish Sharma, I told them. The wedding was going to be in Suva on April 27, 2003.

Neelma and Kunal helped us get to Brisbane International Airport.

As we rode the escalator to international departures, I was laughing so hard I dropped my hand luggage. It went ass over end to the bottom of the escalator. I nearly fell down after it.

The kids thought it was hilarious.

When we arrived in Fiji, I spent my days relaxing at our house in Namadi Heights. We also visited Kavin's mother and enjoyed a meal at the Tradewinds Hotel, where Neelma had previously worked.

Neelma was in charge, I told police. She was 24, Kunal 18, and Sidhi 12. Their big sister, Archana, 26, lived 10 minutes away. I left them cooked meals; lamb and chicken curry, butter chicken and roti.

I gave Sidhi $20 to go shopping.

'But Mum,' she'd protested, 'I have to get you a birthday present and a

Mother's Day present, I need more money!'

I was easily swayed and handed her another $50.

We'd spoken to the children several times after we first arrived, about parties, their work, and Easter.

Neelma was due to have her fourth job interview with Flight Centre the following week. Similar to her flight attendant job with Emirates, recruitment was a multi-interview process. She loved working in the travel industry and this was her dream job; booking and selling holidays to people.

'I'm going to get it!' she told me confidently. 'They wouldn't take me this far if they didn't like me!'

Kunal also told me how he'd accidentally set off the house alarm.

'You know how hard it is to get them out of bed, Ma...well, this had Neelma up in 10 seconds,' he laughed.

'We've had a great life,' I told police. 'So many wonderful memories.'

I spoke of our house, the businesses, our first marriages and watching the children grow up.

I discussed our love of entertaining and travel. 'December was always very busy with both Neelma's and Archana's birthdays, Christmas and New Year's,' I explained.

I also told them about the affairs and assault. It's not something I spoke about often and it pained me to say it aloud.

They wanted to know if Vijay was violent; if he'd ever hurt me. I told them how Vijay assaulted me after we attended the wedding of a friend in 1985, four years after we married.

It wasn't the first time he'd hit me—that had come months earlier - but it was definitely the worst yet. He punched me repeatedly with closed fists, leaving me with a black eye, bruising, and a cut lip.

For someone to curl their fists, look you square in the eye, and hit you was soul destroying. Let alone someone you called your husband and the father of your children. I didn't deserve that; nobody does.

Vijay also strayed regularly from our marriage; I told them. With women he met at work, the shop, or even family members.

In mid-1994, following the death of his father, Vijay travelled back to Fiji. Per visa requirements, Vijay was required to stay in Australia for two years and travelling to Fiji broke this agreement. When he went to return to

Australia, he was refused entry.

He later called me.

'This is my punishment,' he explained. 'This is what I get for betraying you. I've been cheating on you for years and this is what I get for it.'

At first, I didn't believe him. Then he started naming his dirty little secrets.

Among them was the wife of one of my nephews.

I think that one hurt the most.

I had helped this lady when she was down and out, paying for her secretarial course and assisting her with a job looking after the books at Unique Motor Parts. I had even told Vijay to give her a flat to live in at the business address.

On the weekends, she and her husband would come and stay with us at our house on Salato Road. We'd spend hours watching television, cooking together, and picnicking.

Despite his dalliances, I assisted Vijay in reapplying for his return visa to Australia.

To many it may seem strange that I stuck around, but to me, this was something I was accustomed to. It came with the territory of being married and I had to raise my children the best way I could.

This was the first of many visits to that station, and many hours of questioning and statements.

We had only touched briefly on the state of our marriage. There was so much more to tell.

The police never did tell us what happened to our children that day.

We learned that from the media and family.

Our beautiful Nim, Kunal, and Sidhi were with Lord Shiva.

Vijay and I knew we were suspects.

However, even in those early days, we were sure who had murdered our children: Max Sica.

CHAPTER 8

THE WALK-THROUGH

On April 25, 2003, Max was led through our home by Detective Sergeant Zitny. It was three days since he had found our children's bodies and the visit was part of the investigation, police explained.

Dressed in white gloves and blue scrubs, he snuffled and snorted, wiped at his nose. He cried crocodile tears as he was led between the children's bedrooms upstairs. He refused to enter Neelma's room.

The walk-through took just over two hours, the police recording Max's every move.

I saw footage of the walk-through a few years later. I hated seeing him in our house. It made me feel sick.

From very early on, Max was the main person of interest. However, he was never named as a suspect.

We were all 'persons of interest.'

The following is the statement given to police by Max Sica on April 22, 2003:

I am currently unemployed and live at an address known to police.

I came to 20 Grass Tree Close, Bridgeman Downs, so the kids could play and then I was going to invite them to the movies.

I got to the house at about 2:20 pm.

I had been trying to call Neelma all day but was unable to get an answer.

Neelma was expecting me at about 2:30 pm.

I got out of the car with the kids and went to the front door.

I was knocking on the front door. I then tried to call the home phone and Neelma's mobile.

I told my son, Daniel, to look and see if the car was in the garage.

Daniel said it was there along with the dog. I then had a look and saw the Pajero was there. Daniel then went around the back of the house and looked through the back kitchen window to see if anyone was inside.

We were walking back to the fence where we climbed over and I noticed that the rear screen door to the garage was unlocked.

I checked the door and noticed that it was also unlocked.

I didn't go in as the kids were with me.

I then rang the home phone again and got no answer.

I then told the kids to go to the car so that I could go inside.

I gave Daniel my two mobile phones and sunglasses.

I waited until the kids left and then I opened the rear garage door.

When I opened the door the dog came out.

I went inside and picked up a big wooden spoon from behind the garage door as I thought someone may be inside.

I thought this as Neelma always keeps the door locked unless she's having a cigarette. I then walked inside to the laundry door and opened it.

I called out but there was no answer.

I checked around downstairs but didn't see anyone.

As I was looking, I was calling out 'Nim'. I checked all the rooms but the office which is at the front of the house.

While I was downstairs I could smell a bad smell but didn't know what it was. The smell wasn't strong but it was there.

I then went upstairs and the dog was just in front of me. As I got to the top of the stairs I saw blood on the carpet. It was like a streak in front of me.

I then ran straight to Nim's room after I saw the blood. Nim's room was to my right side.

Once I got into Nim's room I saw more blood on the floor.

I then went around the bed to see if she was on the floor but she wasn't there.

The dog was sniffing at the blood on the floor. I could hear a tap running and it was coming from Nim's mum's room.

This room is on the opposite side to Nim's, straight across the road.

I saw another streak of blood on the carpet and there was a remote control on the floor near the blood.

I went into the bathroom that runs off this bedroom.

I saw blankets in the bath and there was water all over the floor. I went in and used the spoon to lift the blankets.

When I lifted the blanket I saw a person's hand.

I turned the tap off. I then pulled out all the blankets and pillows that were in the bathtub. When I was pulling out the blankets Nim's hand touched my hand.

I grabbed her hand and had a look at it.

Her hand was cold and she was all wrinkly.

I could see her chest and what looked like blood.

She was wearing a shirt but I was able to see her breasts. I could also see Nim's brother, Kunal, and Nim's sister, Sidhi, lying in the bath.

Nim was on top. I don't know if the others were clothed. I then just stood there in shock.

I went and washed my face in the other bathroom and then I rang 000 from my mobile twice but got hung up on.

I then used the upstairs home phone but while I was on the home phone my mobile phone rang. It was the police so I hung up the home phone.

I was speaking to the police on the mobile but the reception was not good so I went down the stairs and outside to get a better reception.

I went back inside a couple of times but then the police officer told me not to go back in. I then waited for the police.

— **Excerpt of interview with Constable Daniel Bonwick, District Response Team** [12]

From April 22 to April 25, 2003, Max was interviewed multiple times by police. He was also interviewed on March 31 and April 1, 2004.

On each occasion he was advised he had the right to speak with a solicitor, friend, or relative, that the conversation was being recorded, and that the recording could be used as evidence at a later date.

Max's father, Carlo, sat in on some of the interviews. At some point, Carlo also engaged a solicitor for Max.

In one particular interview, Detective Sergeant Zitny asked Max who he thought was responsible for our children's murders.

'I'm telling you God...is my answer.... My answer is God is responsible for this,' he said.

When Detective Sergeant Zitny suggested Max may be involved, he said no. [13]

He then said, 'I love the question you ended on.' [14]

It was always a game to him.

CHAPTER 9

MAX

Detective Superintendent (then Sergeant) Andrew Massingham started on the case on April 25, 2003, after 16 years in the force, including eight as a detective working in drug squad, prostitution, and property crime. With only 12 months' experience in homicide, he was the new kid on the block. Alongside Detective Sergeant (later Detective Senior Sergeant) Joe Zitny, he eventually took a lead role on the case. Andrew agreed to be interviewed for this book to give his insight on the case, the people, and the investigation. Excerpts of those interviews are included throughout.

"Max was street smart, with a psychopath profile. He was extremely charming and polite and girls were very attracted to him. He was the type that would open the car door for a girl. The way he would talk and parade himself was a cleverly staged act that most women would fall for. When it came to committing the murders, he not only committed the crime to kill them but also for the long-term detriment of those that survived. He manipulated things to hurt his victims."
— Andrew Massingham

Neelma was 22 when she was robbed at knifepoint while working at the Pacific International Hotel in Brisbane as a guest services agent on July 21, 2001.

She was approached from behind by two masked robbers as she worked. She activated the security alarms and chased the assailants away. While not badly hurt, she was understandably shaken. We all were! I hated hearing that she'd been put in such a scary situation. She was taken to the police station and hospital.

With Vijay overseas, and Neelma and I not knowing what to do, I called Carlo for assistance. A warm, caring, and nurturing person, he was happy to help.

When Neelma returned from the hospital, she went to visit Carlo to thank him.

Max was there.

He had just been released on parole after another prison stint and was on home detention at his parents' house.

We'd also heard Sara had left him.

'He can only travel between his house and his sister Rosanna's. He has an ankle bracelet monitoring his movements as well,' Neelma said.

'Are you scared of Max?' I'd asked.

'No,' Neelma replied. 'He didn't do anything wrong, mum. He had drugs planted on him. I trust him. I believe him, and he's been so helpful with everything going on in my life lately.'

I wasn't so sure.

As Neelma explained her injuries to Carlo and Max, including a sore back, Max convinced her that there could be a 'silver lining' to the incident.

'You should sue the hotel,' Max said. 'You should show them you can't work. Tell them you have post-traumatic stress disorder.'

I knew Neelma didn't have this, and she did too.

But Max still gave her details for a doctor.

'Don't do that, Neelma,' I pleaded. 'Don't take people's money for no reason. It's not fair, and it's not what our family does.'

Neelma didn't return to her job at the Pacific International, and she didn't listen to me either. She raised a WorkCover claim against the Pacific International Hotel for $35,000, which was later settled for an amount of $14,345.61.

Max started spending much more time around our family following the Pacific International incident.

When I'd return from shopping, he'd jump the fence to help me with the groceries. On other occasions he'd offer to mow the lawn or take the bins out.

Max and Neelma were also spending much more time together and he started taking Neelma, Kunal, and Sidhi to his parents' restaurant for dinner.

I had concerns about his intentions. So did Vijay.

'He's fake,' Vijay would say. 'Pretending to be something he's not.'

In late 2001, Max brought his kids over to play billiards in our rumpus room at Stafford Heights.

As Vijay and Kunal played a game of pool, Max started talking about drugs—hashish, in particular.

'It's the most potent form of cannabis,' he explained. 'It's also the purest.'

In Vijay's opinion, Max knew too much about drugs. Vijay didn't like him being in the house, and he especially hated Max being around the children.

He didn't trust him, and neither did I.

In spite of this, Max started to visit our house more frequently.

When I raised it with Neelma she told me not to worry. She assured me he was treating her well, that they had a lot in common, and that they had fun together.

During one of Max's visits, Vijay found them sitting at the computer, late at night. This angered him.

'Under no circumstances should Neelma be sitting side by side with a man late at night, in our house,' Vijay yelled. 'Particularly a man with Max's background. I don't want that man in our house anymore.'

The following is part of a statement from Vijay Singh, as included in a Queensland Police Service Statement of Witness: November 11, 2004

'Neelma had become good friends with Max and he would come over and check the computer. I recall one night in our old house at Trouts Road when I got pretty upset after noticing that Max had come over and was sitting with Neelma at the computer in our television area upstairs. He was sitting beside her on another chair. It was night-time and everybody else was going to sleep and Max was still sitting there trying to teach her on the computer. I did not like the idea because my daughter was grown up. She was sitting with a man, late, doing something on the computer. I did not talk to Max on this occasion. I got pretty upset at my wife Shirley and Neelma about this. It was pretty late, after 10:00 pm or so. I told Neelma that I didn't like the idea of her sitting closely with a man. I started talking in loud voices to Neelma and told my wife Shirley that she was supposed to be telling Neelma as a mother that it was time to go to sleep. Max left the house as I was getting upset. Neelma was yelling back at me and the next thing Max comes back to the house and starts knocking on

my front door. I was surprised. He was in a rage. He was saying, 'Neelma, are you alright?' There were no exchanges between Max and I. Neelma's behaviour on this occasion was not in accordance with our customs and beliefs. We protect our children, particularly girls, that they don't go out or establish a relationship until they tell us they want to marry a guy. To my knowledge there was no relationship between Neelma and Max at that time. I was just uncomfortable about what was going on. I have nothing against a guy who is not part of our culture, but we teach our children to appreciate the faiths and beliefs of our Indian culture.'

CHAPTER 10

A CAREER LADY

Neelma always wanted to work as a businesswoman, a mindset she gained from her father.

Following her 21st birthday in 1999, she flew to Fiji to work as a training duty manager at the Raffles Tradewinds Hotel and Convention Centre.

She later travelled to Dunk Island, off Queensland's northeast coast, to gain hands-on experience at the island's resort in international tourism and hospitality.

The island was once used by the Royal Australian Air Force during World War II[15] and was surrounded by reefs and popular with tourists and honeymooners. On a trip to visit her in June 2000, we went snorkelling and swimming and enjoyed a 'booze cruise' on the Barrier Reef, where we spent hours drifting at sea while downing glasses of champagne.

We laughed, cried. She even tricked her friends into thinking her dad was professional golfer, Vijay Singh.

'When your husband goes to a presentation, do you go with him?' her friends had questioned me. 'Like, if he's playing in the US Open, do you travel with him to America?'

'If Vijay Singh, the golfer, was my husband, I would own this island!' I laughed.

Dunk Island Resort was later severely damaged by Cyclone Larry in March 2006 and destroyed in Cyclone Yasi in 2011. I was devasted to see it gone, I made such fond memories there.

Following her work on the island, Neelma applied for job as a flight attendant with Emirates Airline in Dubai.

'Mum, I'm going to get this job!' she assured me after several interviews. 'I can take you to Paris, and to India.'

She was clearly overjoyed with her decision. We'd taught the kids to be independent and travel the world so I was excited for her.

Neelma interviewed four times for the flight attendant job at the then-Gazebo Hotel in Brisbane. When she got her fifth interview, with only eleven girls left, I realised the complexity of the situation. I knew there was every chance she was going to get the job and leave me again.

'I'll start with three months of training in Dubai before I'll be officially enrolled as an air hostess,' she explained. 'After I finish the Emirates training, I'll return to Australia and work for an Australian aviation company.'

I was so happy for her.

I also knew Dubai was an opportunity to split Max and her up.

After all, that is why Neelma had split with her last boyfriend.

Neelma had met Amit Lala when she was 19 and they'd dated for three years. He was a student accountant, the cousin of Archana's boyfriend Kavin and from a well-respected Indian family.

While Vijay didn't approve of Neelma seeing a man out of wedlock, he agreed he was a nice boy.

On the day Neelma and Amit split, Amit stood outside our house crying while she threw his possessions at him, and in the bin.

It actually made me very sad.

We'd heard his family was worried about Neelma's international work; they thought Amit might move overseas to be with her.

I knew she was heartbroken after splitting with Amit, but Max's shoulder wasn't the right one to cry on.

'You're going to be amazing in Dubai,' I told her. 'I'm so proud of you.'

Neelma flew to Dubai on February 21, 2002. Vijay travelled back from Fiji to help her get ready to go overseas, and to say goodbye. Just before she left, Vijay bought her a new laptop computer to take with her.

'It will help you keep in touch with everyone,' Vijay assured.

Max installed the computer software and readied the computer for her to use. In some ways, I feel Max let her go so she could get the training to earn as much money as possible in Brisbane.

After all, he always made sure there was something in it for him. A little sweetener; a cherry on top.

I was certain he was a crook but it was also very clear there was nothing

I could do to stop their relationship from forming; I just had to trust in Neelma's judgement. Trust that she'd realise his true character before it was too late, that she'd choose someone very special to spend the rest of her life with and that she wouldn't choose that person to be Max.

In March 2002, Neelma had a fight with one of her roommates—a French girl—while at Emirates training school. After Neelma smelled marijuana on her roommate while riding the hotel lift, a fight ensued. I never instilled that sort of behaviour in my children, but Neelma was feisty and passionate. She later told me she was scared of her roommate, and worried she would lose her job because of her.

'You can't live in a country like the United Arab Emirates, take drugs, and get away with it,' Neelma said.

Around this same there was an incident at our Bridgeman Downs home that would cause irreparable damage to the Singh–Sica family relationship.

With Neelma still overseas, and construction on our house nearing completion, Max paid Vijay a visit.

Joining Vijay in our new garage, which was peppered with leftover bricks, paint, and building offcuts, he shook his hand.

'Papa, there's something I want to ask you. I'm in love with Neelma and I want to marry her—'

Vijay cut him off. He'd already heard enough. He didn't like this man and he certainly didn't want him marrying his beautiful Neelma.

'I don't approve of your relationship,' Vijay explained. 'Look at yourself. You've been in jail. You have two children. You're Italian. You're divorced.'

Max's face reddened, his eyes raged.

Vijay was equally angered. How dare this man assume the hand of Neelma!

'Leave, or I will smash you to pieces,' Vijay screamed, arming himself with a brick.

'You don't know what I'm capable of. I'll bring you down,' Max countered.

Carlo later warned Vijay about Max's capabilities.

'He has a good knowledge of martial arts,' Carlo said, but Vijay wasn't fazed.

* * *

We moved into our new home on April 11, 2002. I could not wait to show Neelma through the place when she was home.

CHAPTER 11

RELATIONSHIPS SOUR

In April 2002, Vijay received Neelma's telephone bill and noticed a familiar number.

It was Max's.

She had recently sworn they were no longer speaking. Vijay was so angry. Max wasn't the right person for Neelma, and Vijay knew it. I knew it. We all knew it.

'He's not the man for you, Neelma. He's not welcome in our family,' Vijay told her.

Neelma left her aviation course with Emirates and secretly returned to Australia on May 3, 2002.

Max greeted her at the airport.

Presumably elated by the gratuitous move, she followed him to his house in Bribie Island, a good 45-minute drive from Brisbane city.

For the next six weeks they lived, hand in hand, as he spun his twisted stories and double-barrelled lies.

On June 16, 2002, as I returned home from Fiji, Kunal greeted me.

'Nim is home,' he said, excitedly. 'She's sleeping.'

True to his words, I found my beautiful Neelma fast asleep in her bed.

My girl was home! For the coming months, she was all mine again. No Max, no worries.

Vijay was also elated.

However, the worst was yet to come.

We started to receive terrible phone calls; mostly prank. Morning, afternoon and night. They filled me with concern and horror.

One of the first was on a Sunday night, not long after we got our weekly

KFC for dinner. Neelma, Kunal, and Sidhi went to pick the food up while I waited at home. I answered the phone on the third ring.

The voice was that of a man. He quickly identified himself as a detective from a local police station.

'The person Neelma is seeing is bad,' he said. 'He is a criminal we have been watching. Neelma has been living with him at Bribie Island. He is not a good person and she deserves better. Trust me.'

The person was quick to hang up.

I felt sick. I wasn't sure if it was a real detective or not, and I wasn't sure what to do with the information.

When the children got back from picking up dinner, I stayed quiet; bit my tongue. I was confused, yes. But I didn't want to cause any problems. Neelma had just got home and I wanted to enjoy her company.

That night, we enjoyed a few glasses of wine. After we cleaned and washed up. I told Neelma I had something important to ask her. Kunal, who was listening in, yelled out.

'I told you not to hide anything from Mama.'

Neelma seemed slightly concerned, before composing herself.

'Mum, I learned a lot about this man while living with him. I sat next to him while he hacked his friend's computer. He is so clever with that technical stuff,' she said.

He also told her he was planning to kidnap an Asian businessman from a shopping centre in the southern suburbs of Brisbane, for money.[16]

'He's planning the kidnapping with his friends,' she said. 'He's part of a gang.'

The plan was to drag the man into a disabled toilet at the Sunnybank centre where they would use a stun gun to disable him, redress him, put him in a wheelchair, and put a blanket over him. They would then put tanning lotion on him and a hat and wheel him outside into a van. Afterwards, they'd take him to a house at Mount Tamborine—on the Gold Coast—where they would ask for a large ransom.

As I would later find out, Max reported all of this to police. He apparently hoped to have his parole reduced, and framed his friends so he could 'dob' them in to score brownie points.

Of course, Neelma swore me to secrecy and all of this information was highly confidential. She explained he was a dangerous man, and that she would break things off with him slowly.

'Max told me he could wear a balaclava at night and stand right in our yard and we wouldn't even know he was there.

'He also told me he had the capability to switch off the home alarm system and tap into our home phone through his car radio.'

Her stories worried me, and I told her to be careful.

I think Max realised she was going to break up with him, and this was his way of controlling her, of scaring her.

With her ex-partner Amit, Neelma was nice and respectable, with a great attitude.

With Max she didn't give a damn about anyone or anything.

She didn't show him respect and he didn't have any for her either.

In my opinion it was a physical connection, not an emotional one. She was heartbroken over Amit and Max was the shoulder to cry on.

CHAPTER 12

A BAD HUSBAND

Detective Senior Sergeant Bryan Paton was stationed at the Criminal Investigation Branch at Petrie Police Station when the Singh children were murdered. Bryan agreed to be interviewed for this book, sharing his thoughts on Shirley, Vijay, and Max. Excerpts of those interviews are included throughout. Bryan retired from the Queensland Police Service in December 2004.

'Shirley took nine months to tell us about the prostitutes and swingers clubs. She was an absolute basket case when she finished the story, an emotional wreck. That type of behaviour went against everything Shirley believed in. She thought we would think less of her because of it ... that we would hate her for it. She knew the importance of telling us everything and she agonised over that.'
—**Bryan Paton**

Vijay was always very quick to react if he wasn't happy and things would regularly turn physical.

As the patriarch of our family, the provider and protector, Vijay ruled with an iron fist. His Fijian affairs become more and more common, and my knowledge of them, greater.

However, despite his physical and emotional abuse, I wanted the kids to have a father. I always thought about the children's pleasure, comfort, and finances before my own. I wanted my children to enjoy the best things in life and Vijay gave us that.

They attended good schools, wore good clothes, and enjoyed regular outings to theme parks and restaurants.

Vijay was close with all his children, but particularly close with Neelma.

She appreciated him as a father, and how hard he worked for the family. That bond was something that existed for much of Neelma's life.

Neelma was particularly good at cooking, baking, roasting, and decorating. She made the most amazing passionfruit upside-down cake, which was Vijay's favourite. However, this didn't always agree with his health. As a type 2 diabetic, Vijay has to monitor what he eats, and takes tablets to regulate his blood sugar levels.

Whenever Neelma wanted to make him a cake, I'd advise her against it. My warning would almost always fall on deaf ears though. I'd regularly smell the sweet, spicy essence of that passionfruit cake drifting through the house.

I'd come out of my room, shaking my head, my arms folded.

'But mum, I used Splenda!' she'd say, laughing.

My children never lacked anything. I made up my mind very early on that no matter what, I wouldn't be selfish and I would do anything for them.

Worried about the future of our marriage, I decided to return to the workforce. I felt it necessary to gain skills, and I also hoped it would help our relationship.

I started working as a massage therapist at Clear Mountain Lodge on Brisbane's northside, and later as a therapeutic massage practitioner at the Academy of Natural Health in Brisbane. I underwent training in Polynesian Ka Huna, Swedish, remedial, and deep tissue massage, waxing, eyelash and eyebrow tinting, and acrylic nails.

I later opened my own beauty and massage business, House of Relaxation, at our home in Bridgeman Downs.

Despite successes in my working life, things at home were getting worse. Vijay started asking me to take part in more sordid affairs. He wanted me to participate in a threesome and said he wouldn't cheat on me with anyone else if I obliged.

This made me feel very uncomfortable. Not only was this against our vows as husband and wife but against my morals as well.

Out of my 36 male cousins, only two had cheated on their wives. And none had ever hit their wives, that I knew of.

In the Hindu religion, women were considered to be Lakshmi, the goddess of wealth, fortune, and prosperity.[17] So, if a man was to treat his wife badly, she could potentially leave. And, as a result, financial privileges/wealth would be taken away from the man's family.

Concerned about the consequences, I consulted my cousin, a Hindu religious teacher referred to as Swami.

He told me nothing between a husband and wife was a sin, and that it may be the only way of keeping my family together.

So, when Vijay told me he was hiring a prostitute to come to our house at Stafford Heights on a Saturday night in late 1994, I felt I had no choice.

After the children went to sleep, Vijay prepared the downstairs rumpus room for a visitor.

I drank half a bottle of Johnnie Walker Red, to ensure I was really drunk.

When Vijay went to the toilet, and recognising my concern and lack of interest, the prostitute promised not to touch me.

When Vijay returned from the bathroom, they had sex. I couldn't watch; I felt physically sick, dirty.

The next day, I couldn't stop crying. I didn't go near our prayer room for a couple of days afterwards.

Vijay ordered prostitutes another two times to our Stafford Heights home. I was sickened both times.

On the weekends, Vijay would take me to swingers' bars and clubs in Brisbane city. In particular, he loved visiting a well-known late-night swingers' bar in an industrial area of inner-city Brisbane. The club had a BYO bar with red leather lounges and a powder room with costumes. There was a shadow screen for couples, stripper poles, private booths, and a dance floor. Porn played on large-screen televisions and private rooms allowed guests to have sex behind closed doors.

While he acquainted himself with fellow club-goers, I'd spend my time getting drunk at the bar.

It had come to the point where I didn't even care what he did. In fact, it might sound stupid, but I don't even really know what Vijay was doing half the time at those clubs. We'd never bring anyone home and he'd never force me to do anything with anyone. He just wanted me with him.

Any opportunity to go out was a good one for me ... even if that meant being introduced to the seedy underworld of swinging sex parties in the backstreets of Brisbane.

He continued to beat me too. In 1995, after an argument about him sleeping around, he dragged me along the carpet by my hair and punched me in the face. Neelma called the police, who locked him up in a cell for the night.

I was transported to the Royal Brisbane and Women's Hospital, where they treated the carpet burns with ointment and placed a pad over my black eye. They couldn't do anything for my bruised jaw.

I remember feeling saddened I was silly enough to anger him. Not angry that he'd been stupid enough to hurt me.

Around the same time, I started drinking heavily while the kids were at school; mainly scotch. I think I was depressed and trying to numb my pain.

I didn't accept what Vijay did to me, and I was prepared to leave him.

Archana and Neelma suspected something was wrong and called on my sister-in-law, Margaret, to check in on me. Of course, I was drunk and started crying as soon as I saw her.

We spoke for hours. 'If your finger gets a sore, you heal the sore, not cut off your finger,' Margaret said. 'He provides well for the children; you have a nice home ... he's overseas most of the time. Don't cut him off.'

To me, that meant working at our relationship.

The following is an excerpt from The Courier-Mail (Mark Oberhardt) on March 3, 2012.[18]

Barrister Sam Di Carlo, for Sica, asked questions about the sexual encounters Shirley Singh and her husband Vijay Singh had in the 1990s.

Mr Di Carlo asked if Vijay Singh had admitted to his wife that he had been having sexual affairs around 1994.

'He wasn't having affairs, he was having flings, Mr Di Carlo,' Shirley Singh said.

She went on to explain that Vijay Singh had asked her about having sex with other people and to watch pornographic videos because it would excite him.

Mr Di Carlo asked if Vijay Singh had told her she would be failing in her role as a wife if she didn't take part.

'Yeah, I think my husband said that,' Shirley Singh replied.

She said she was aware Vijay had used an adult shop contact magazine to get a woman and then a man to come to their original home at Stafford for sex.

Mr Di Carlo also asked questions about a series of assaults by Vijay Singh on Shirley Singh during their marriage.

He asked if Shirley Singh had received a black eye, bruising to the left side of her face and a cut lip.

'Something did happen about 26 years ago, (but) is it relevant to what has happened to my children? It was in Fiji?' Shirley Singh asked.

She hadn't gone to police because it would have made things worse and she had been raised to sort things out at home.

Mr Di Carlo asked whether she had told police Vijay Singh had assaulted her about 50 times over the years.

'We have been married about 35 years, I think 50 is not too bad,' Shirley Singh replied.

CHAPTER 13

IDENTIFICATION

Shirley's love for her children permeated everything; it was her whole existence. I didn't know Shirley prior to the murders. However, the fact she now had three dead children was like a shroud. It didn't matter what conversation I had with her, it always come back to the children. Her dreams, what had happened and what they might have said to her in them. There would be laughter, tears and anger. Her whole life revolved around her children; there wasn't much she wouldn't do for those kids. She'd have sold her soul to the devil if it meant those kids would be OK. Her whole reason for being was because of her kids … that became even more apparent when they died.

—**Bryan Paton**

Four days after our children were discovered, Vijay and I were asked to identify their bodies.

Our beautiful, innocent, gorgeous children.

The children I'd raised, fed, and bathed. Whose little noses would scrunch when they laughed, and whose cuddles made even the cloudiest of days sunny. They'd grown into strong and fierce individuals, choosing their own likes and dislikes, ambitions and dreams.

They'd always been there for me; in the good times, and the bad.

Like any family, we had our ups and downs but were incredibly protective of each other.

Neelma was dignified, courageous, ambitious, caring, and loving. She always stood by me and always protected me. She was a sister and friend, as well as a daughter.

Kunal was gentle, kind, and caring. He had a huge sense of humour, always making everyone laugh, and was a little bit cheeky. Ambitious and creative, he wanted to be a designer. He decided to do a business major first though so he could help his father with the latest technology. He would rub his chin on my cheeks and say you're the best mum in the whole wide world.

Sidhi was my baby. She always clung to me. She wanted to be a singer and would sing songs from the movie 'Titanic' constantly. I remember once telling her to leave me alone, as I was busy. I regretted that now she was gone for good.

Police laid forensic photos of Neelma, Kunal, and Sidhi in front of me before wheeling their bodies out one by one. They were on a cold aluminium trolley, their bodies covered by only a sheet.

Nothing can prepare you for that.

I wanted to spew. I felt cold.

I dabbed at my forehead and eyes with a crumpled tissue. My vision was blurred and my mouth was dry.

I grasped at the railings, the windows, the wall ... I ripped at my fingernails with anxiety. I willed my body to stay upright; police holding me tight.

'Why?' I wailed. 'Why my babies? They were so small.'

The lights were bright, the room spinning.

I felt hot. My skin hurt.

My clothes were tight. I clawed at my top. I felt strangled.

'This isn't real. That's *not* them. Who did this? A monster.'

I then saw Sidhi. I hit the floor.

My brother Jayant called Sidhi grasshopper while my brother Turbert referred to her as sparrow. She was never in one place and always jumping around.

And yet here she was, motionless.

Someone very sadistic and cruel had done this to them.

Where had I gone wrong for this to happen?

I used to think the same when Vijay cheated.

Had I not cooked well enough, was the house not clean enough? What did I do to deserve this? What did they do? They were good children.

I also blamed Vijay.

'This is your fault. For cheating, for hitting me, for hurting the children,' I screamed. '*You* did this. *You* caused this grief.'

Shock.

Loss.

Anger.

Guilt.

Regret.

Pain.

Sadness.

Loneliness.

Fear.

That was our lives now.

The following were the findings from pathologist Dr Alex Olumbe:

Neelma's primary cause of death was manual strangulation. She also suffered three vertical, symmetrical lacerations on her forehead which could have been made by a garden fork found at the house.

Kunal died from drowning after sustaining a head injury which left him unconscious. He had an injury to the side of his head which may have been caused by a garden fork.

Sidhi's cause of death was determined as a head injury sustained by 'severe force' with a blunt instrument. She had three symmetrical lacerations on the side of her head consistent with being caused by a garden fork.

CHAPTER 14

RETURNING HOME

'When you go into a house where there has been a murder, there is a feeling to it. It's very real, and there is a feeling of life energy no longer being there. There's a feeling of darkness. With time, the darkness, grief, and evil rub off on you. And that shade never really leaves you. I really got a sense of that working on this case. I'd never had that feeling before.'
—**Bryan Paton**

One week after the children's bodies were found, Vijay and I returned to our Bridgeman Downs home for the first time.

Media were camped out the front and police tape cordoned the yard from public entry. A number of orange traffic cones lined the house, illuminated under the autumn sun like a wall of fire.

Seeing the house made me feel sick. It reminded me of the children. We'd been so excited to move there.

As I was led from the car, up our driveway, and through the front doors, I was scared what I was going to see. I didn't know what to expect.

Police asked me to describe anything that looked out of the ordinary.

Our mop, one of those ones with loose strands that you have to wring out, was standing up in the garage near the internal door. We always kept it lying down on the barbecue in the garage to dry.

I also noticed that it was tightly squeezed.

There was also a red bucket on the laundry floor, half filled with dirty water.

Vijay's and my laundry basket was downstairs; we always kept it in the master bedroom.

KFC boxes were on the kitchen bench; police said they had removed them from the bin.

The dishes had been washed and were stacked in the dryer, just like Neelma always did.

The light above our kitchen table was kinked and falling from the ceiling, the roof above it swollen. There was also a large hole and cracks, which split the ceiling like black zippers from one end to the other. The police explained that water from the spa bath had got into the air conditioning ducts.

I was then taken upstairs. I was numb.

Everything was so clean, strangely clean. Given the damage to their bodies and the obvious struggle they had encountered with their murderer, it struck me as odd.

As I reached the last stairs, I saw red marks coming from Neelma's and Kunal's rooms towards my room.

'What's that?' I asked the police.

'That's what we're trying to determine,' the police said.

I realised it was probably blood but was surprised by how light it was.

We walked into Kunal's room first. I noticed an old green blanket underneath his bed. This was usually on the top shelf of the linen cupboard. His bed was a mess, with blood spots on the side he always slept.

We next travelled to the main bathroom, where I noticed a decorative figurine missing.

Next, we went into Neelma's room. Her jewellery box was on the floor, upside down and empty. A painted stone, gold necklace, earrings, bracelets, bangles, rings, and pendants were all missing.

'Police investigating the scene of the crime found Neelma had items of jewellery stolen. This included about four pairs of 22ct gold earrings. However, Max only took one of each of the pair of earrings. To me that said he wanted the parents to know the killer had the other earring. He wanted the parents to have that final memory of their daughter—for them to be constantly reminded of the killer. That's the mentality of the bloke; that's how he operates.'

—Andrew Massingham

Also missing were Neelma's diary, her camera, and four or five photos of Amit.

Neelma had kept a diary for as long as I could remember. She'd write in it nightly, before bed. Her 2003 diary was the only one missing. Her old ones were still in her drawer, in the bedroom. Not long before she died, she told me she had been writing about Max in her diary.

In Sidhi's room, I noticed her purse with her house key was missing as well as a plush toy tiger.

I was led into my room last. I saw blood.

I knew straight away Sidhi had slept in our room that night, something she often did.

All of my cupboards were open. Strangely, my jewellery box was on my duchess, untouched.

I was taken to our ensuite last. A large wooden spoon, which I used to stir my cooking, was sitting on the floor beside our spa bath.

'Why is that there?' I asked the police.

Like almost every question I asked them that day, and for the months and years that followed, it went unanswered.

I was so upset and sick when I left the house that day. I was hurting so bad.

A few days earlier, Max had walked the police through our home.

It was he who had discovered the bodies, in a bath full of hot running water in the upper level of our five-bedroom home.

They weren't shot, as first reported. They had been mutilated.

Max had bypassed inch-deep water and blood-soaked carpet as he climbed the stairs of our family home to discover the three bodies of my beautiful children, covered by a doona in the spa bath of our ensuite.

This was a man that had been in prison before, a man that knew you should never cross a crime scene boundary.

From the moment he'd entered the house and saw running water from the overflowing upstairs bath, he should have called police.

But no. He retrieved a large wooden spoon from our garage. He walked upstairs and crossed over bloodied marks on the carpet. He then used that spoon to peel back the doona that swamped their bludgeoned bodies and push them further under the murky water.

CHAPTER 15

THE FUNERAL

On May 10, 2003, the police handed our house back.

Vijay and Archana returned to the house first. I went later.

The upstairs was still boarded up while forensic investigations were undertaken. Renovations also had to be completed. They were going to cost $180,000.

Not hearing my children's laughter, their chatter, their big and little feet moving around the house, was devastating.

However, it was important we were there as on May 14 we would farewell our children.

As part of the Hindu religion, the last prayers for the deceased always occur in the home, before the place of cremation.

My half-brother from Fiji, Swami Ram Naresh, a well-respected priest, would perform these.

We threw mattresses on the ground and slept between the lounge room and rumpus.

Others stayed on our sofa, or in the massage room.

On May 14 I woke excited to bring my children home. Can you imagine that? I'm off to their funeral—to farewell their spirits to a greater place—and here I was excited to 'be' with them, just one more time.

My friend Elizabeth, her partner, Olly, and my sisters from Fiji and Auckland were all staying with us.

I dressed in a green and black silk sari, gifted to me by Archana and Neelma during a trip to Singapore years earlier. Vijay wore white and his head was shaven, as per Hindu custom in mourning.

At 11 am, three black hearses arrived at our house, each carrying the body of one of my children.

We provided police with a list of family and friends attending, and the entrance to our estate was blocked to all others. Several dozen undercover officers roamed the streets around the house.

Vijay and I, along with Swami Ram Naresh and his wife, Sunita, gathered in the rumpus room. The three coffins were laid in front of us by the funeral directors and the door closed to the rest of the house.

There is no way to easily express how I felt.

My children's dead bodies were in my house and I was saying goodbye to them for the final time.

I never thought I would experience something like this in my lifetime.

It was soul destroying.

Everything I'd gone through in life—adoption, cheating, abuse—was nothing compared to this.

When you welcome children into the world, you do so with an unspoken promise to love and protect them for life.

In ways, I felt like I'd failed them.

That I'd failed as a mother.

I would never get to cuddle them again, to laugh with them or to dream with them.

When we completed the prayers, the coffins were taken back to the hearses. Detective Senior Sergeant Bryan Paton drove us to the cemetery in my maroon Pajero.

The funeral was arranged by my brother Turbert, in consultation with the Queensland Police. My only job was to choose the flowers that would adorn the caskets.

Red roses for Kunal as he'd always given these to his girlfriend Katrina. He also once presented me with a dozen long-stem roses after crashing my car in the rain.

Red roses for Neelma as her favourite colour was red.

And frangipanis for Sidhi. We used to have a frangipani tree in the front yard of our house in Stafford Heights and Sidhi would often make garlands for her hair, neck, and arms. She loved their smell and their colour.

The funeral was held in the main chapel of the crematorium.

Camphor was lit in formation along the pathway, illuminating a path for the coffins to the church.

Police were everywhere, as were mourners – thousands of them, according to media reports.

I didn't even notice them. I couldn't stop crying.

I was helped to the chapel and sat beside Archana, my sisters-in-law Margaret and Pratibha, my sister Trishulla from New Zealand, and my cousin from Auckland Vijay Laxhmi.

My nephew Ronald spoke about Neelma's beauty.

'She should have been a film star,' he said. 'She'd step out of her Mitsubishi FTO, with her Guess sunglasses on and her big smile. You really don't see pretty girls like that every day.'

Kunal's high school principal from St James College, Dr Kerrie Tuite, spoke of his kindness.

'He would always share his amazing Indian food with his teachers,' she said. 'His roti and salmon. Another thing I know for sure ... he loved his mother more than anything.'

The principal from Sidhi's school at Kedron, John Leyden, also spoke.

He said Sidhi was like a butterfly, always happy and always caring for people.

'The children loved her, she always made people laugh,' he said.

The priest also spoke on the day.

Archana was distraught and it was clear that being near me upset her even more. The kids adored their big sister. Even after she had left the home, they were all so close. If Sidhi wanted to go to the movies with her friends, she'd ask Archana for permission first. Sidhi wouldn't always listen to me, but she would always listen to Archana.

Neelma and Archana were also very close. Neelma called Archana 'Bugs Bunny', as her teeth often stuck out in photos.

As the eldest in the family, Archana was well respected and loved. She was a big sook but that is what always made her so special.

From the moment the children's lives were taken, Archana was hurting. She was scared, and she didn't like seeing me upset. Her husband, Kavin, was the same.

Everything was going relatively smoothly at the chapel, until they drew the curtain to take the bodies away.

In Hindu culture, we cremate the bodies. I'm OK with this usually. But my own children, no. If I had it my way, I'd have embalmed them.

As the crematory staff pulled at the curtains, and I watched the coffins start to disappear from view, I jumped.

I ran, my arms outstretched, helpless and saddened.

I wanted to save them.

I was held back by officers.

Later, when we returned from the funeral, I pushed and punched Vijay for allowing them to be cremated.

'How dare you burn our children's bodies, you're disgusting,' I screamed.

Of course, it wasn't his fault. But I was looking for someone to blame, anyone.

Max also attended but was removed by police. His face was splashed across the media that night, cigarette in hand, as he was led by officers across the lawns of the memorial gardens. Such a grub.

The next day Vijay travelled to Nudgee Beach, maybe 20 minutes from ours, where mangroves and bike paths hug the foreshore.

Together with the other men from our families, he let the children's ashes free, enabling their spirits to wander once again.

CHAPTER 16

OUR FAITH

Our religion was incredibly important to us, particularly in those early days.

As devout Hindus, we believed there was one true God, Brahman. In Hinduism, Brahman occupies the highest place, as the creator and enjoyer of all creation.

There are thousands of Gods and Goddesses—known as deity—which represent the many aspects of Brahman.

Each day, we would make personal offerings to the deity.

Vijay, Archana, and I always prayed to Lord Shiva.

Before their deaths, Kunal also prayed to Lord Shiva and the Monkey God, Hanuman – the symbol of strength and energy; Neelma prayed to the Goddess of Strength, Durga; and Sidhi to Lord Krishna, the God of Compassion, Tenderness, and Love.

Following the funeral, we prayed for 13 days.

This was typical of the Hindu religion, where the dead are mourned after cremation.

May 15 was Day 1.

When you are mourning, there is no celebration of food.

In the first ten days we ate only boiled food and no meat.

In fact, many years ago, the person who lit the fire at the cremation would only eat fruit for the first ten days.

Men also don't cut their hair or shave for ten days. Because they are grieving, it's not appropriate to groom themselves.

As women, we would shower and tie our hair up, but I wore no makeup, and did not comb my hair. In fact, I rarely wore makeup in the three years following the children's deaths. I still put on nice clothes but I didn't care what I looked like.

On the tenth, eleventh, twelfth, and thirteenth day after death, a number of rituals are performed in order to mark a return to normal life.

Men shave their face and head, often releasing their hair into the ocean.

We started to eat properly again and also completed a Havan, a religious ceremony in which we dug a sacred fire pit in our backyard and recited Sanskrit mantras.

We delivered food to our children on a banana leaf then sat cross-legged on the lawn around the fire pit, known as the Havan Kund.

On May 26, the thirteenth day of prayers, I woke at 2 am. I was in a really bad state and had slept terribly.

Terahvin—a feast to farewell the dead—is always held on the thirteenth day. Planning a feast for my children's deaths was not something I ever envisioned but it had to be done. I was going to cook them the most amazing feast they had ever seen.

I cooked a potato curry with blue peas, jackfruit curry, pumpkin curry, a split pea curry, bhindi masala (the children's favourite), French beans fried in tomatoes, taro leaf bhaji, spinach curry, raita with cucumber and carrot, and kheer (a rice pudding).

From 4 am, family and friends started arriving to help.

The house was filled with gas stoves, burners, and pots.

As people buzzed around, eager to help, I convinced myself it wasn't the thirteenth day of prayer for my children's deaths but the day of Neelma's wedding instead.

I even mixed together turmeric and oil and rubbed it all over Neelma's photo on the wall.

Turmeric, or haldi, as it's called in India, is seen as a symbol of purity. It is regularly rubbed onto the bride and groom before a wedding in a ceremony called 'mayian.'

Archana was helping cook, but she wasn't in a good state. When I told her it was Neelma's wedding, she lost it at me.

'It's NOT her wedding, Mum!' she screamed. 'It's just not. Neelma's gone. They are all gone. I wasn't there for them. I could have helped,' she whimpered.

I felt Archana's pain and anguish but I was disconnected. I didn't stop to pull her in, or to hold her. I didn't stop to wipe her tears or touch her heart. I didn't ask her if she was OK, and I didn't tell her I loved her.

I didn't give her what she needed in that moment. She later told me she felt very alone.

It was raining cats and dogs that day and in Hindu culture, rain is a heavenly blessing.

It rained on both the funeral and the thirteenth day of prayer.

We had thirteen priests and almost 200 people come over that day.

The police had to control traffic into our estate again, and ensure the security of our home and guests.

I had many sovereign gold coins, which I'd been collecting for my children. Along with money, I gave these to the priests.

In Hindu custom, the children would be helped to heaven by the gifts we gave the priests.

Danam, the ritual of giving gifts in charity, also meant providing the priests with clothes and other items.

After the prayers and food, people started to leave at around 3 or 4 pm. As people departed our house, I began to feel empty. Realisation of the past few weeks started to really set in.

Our house was usually filled with people celebrating birthdays and weddings with us, not mourning the deaths of our children.

Our close relatives stayed with us, including Archana.

I was so emotionally exhausted.

However, I hadn't seen the day as the final goodbye.

Per Hindu culture, it was a year later—during srāddha—that we would say our final goodbyes.

Every year, in September, we mourn for fifteen days—completing our prayers with family, friends, and priests.

I was so mad at Lord Shiva. He was meant to keep my family safe but he didn't. One day, I even removed every idol from my prayer room and placed them outside, scolding the Lord for taking my children from me.

I needed my religion though; it was the only thing that helped keep me sane. It was part of who I was, it was part of my flesh and blood. It gave me purpose and some hope that I could assist the children in being looked after for the rest of their lives in heaven.

The deceased are seen as angels and I now had three more looking after me from above.

CHAPTER 17

THE AFFAIRS

'Vijay was complex and so much harder to get to know than Shirley. He had a dark side. But more than anything he hated the fact we knew about it, that it all came out. He was highly sexed and he'd had affairs. I used to tell Vijay, you need to tell us everything as we will find out in the long run. He didn't show his emotions as much as Shirley and was pretty insular. He adored his children though. He was a bit more pragmatic, and probably loved them in a more disciplined way. He wasn't a horrible human being for what he did. I don't get it and it goes against everything I think and believe but I don't judge him for it.'

—Bryan Paton

In the lead-up to the murders, Vijay's and my relationship had really broken down.

We stopped having sex, and while we would stay in the same room together, I couldn't stand him touching me.

In October of 2002, Vijay returned home from Fiji after one of his trips. He was acting weird. Dancing and talkative, he stopped regularly to take phone calls.

'Papa, what are you doing?' Sidhi demanded. 'Why are you acting so funny?'

'Sid, my little Sid, I'm just having fun,' he exclaimed.

But I knew there was more to it; he was never this happy.

He was acting like a teenager in love. Something was up.

That same day I was feeling very sick and went to the doctor. I felt hot and dizzy, and my feet were swelling.

When I returned from my appointment, we got into an argument.

Neelma warned him to leave me alone. 'Her blood pressure is high!'

'Who cares? She smokes, it's her own fault. Let her die!' Vijay said.

His words cut me to the core. They were horrible and delivered with venom. Distraught, I asked if he'd found someone else.

His answer? Yes.

'Now take the children and fuck off,' he screamed. 'You can have the unit at Rydges South Bank and I'll get my girlfriend to come stay with me in the house.'

How dare he! No way was I giving up my family home.

'You know what, Vijay Singh, you've really done it this time,' I yelled, my heart racing as I spoke. 'You are hurting people. You are chasing me out of this house. One day you will not get to see your children's faces. A time will come where you will long to see their faces and they won't be there for you. You'll die alone.'

As the words left my lips, I wished I'd never said them. They were very hurtful. But that's how mad I was.

As I started to calm, I realised he couldn't just kick me out of my home. He couldn't just bring any girl to Australia to live with him. Australia had a strict immigration policy and I was pretty sure this tart of a woman didn't fit within that.

He was going to lose out, not me.

Afterwards, I discussed this other woman with Neelma. When I'd asked Vijay who she was, he had challenged me to find her. Neelma was convinced we should follow through on this.

'Don't you want to know who she is?' she asked. 'The woman that wants to take over your family home?'

She was right. I did want to know.

We booked our flights that day, and in late October 2002, we flew to Fiji.

* * *

While we searched Fiji for Vijay's woman, Vijay was at home in Australia, oblivious to the fact we had even left the country.

It took him three days to realise we weren't at home, let alone that we'd left Australia. I'm not kidding.

Despite our best intentions to find his new girlfriend, we couldn't easily get the info. Because Vijay was 'the boss,' none of his associates would tell me what he was doing. I decided to search his office.

In the 28 years we'd then been together, I had never once sat in his office chair at his business, or picked up his order book, but this day I did.

I shuffled through the pages, glazing over the scribble for orders of spare parts and office stationery. My eye soon caught on to something out of the ordinary.

An order for a washing machine, gas stove, and iron.

None of these items were in our Fiji home!

I later found orders for furniture, and an unrecognisable number on his phone bill, which I called.

A lady by the name of Karun answered. I identified myself as Vijay's wife and pressed the woman for further information on who she was. She eventually buckled.

'I'm Vijay's girlfriend and we're in love and about to get married,' she told me.

'You can have him, he's all yours,' I said, laughing. As I hung up the phone though, I become angered.

This woman was tearing our family apart.

She too was married, although separated from her husband. And, she was living in a flat paid for by Vijay.

Fancy that. A flat paid for by my husband!

I was outraged.

When I'd previously suspected Vijay was cheating, I'd told him to stop bringing the women to our house.

'Don't you dare bring them in my bed,' I'd say. 'Take them somewhere else.'

So that's what he'd done. Got her a place that he could go to.

We later attempted to confront Karun at the local pizza shop where she worked. However, as we entered the shop at closing time—she spotted us. She ran through the back door and down an alleyway. She jumped into a car, waving her finger at us as she moved.

'You can't have my father. He'll fuck you for three months then show you the door,' Neelma screamed. 'You'll see!'

Given the furniture and electrical items were purchased for the flat with company money, I decided to report the situation to police. I hoped they could help me ask for them back.

I offered the police a bottle of scotch, and they assisted in arranging a meeting between Neelma, myself, and Karun at the station.

Karun sat at a table across from me. She was short, maybe five foot tall, with her hair tied into a bun. She was better looking than I was expecting. Better than the others Vijay usually went for, I reasoned.

She looked scared.

'So what's going on, are you having an affair with my husband?' I asked, launching straight into it.

'Yes, I am. But who cares?' she said.

Rude, indignant, and uncaring.

My anger levels rose and I willed myself to ignore her spoiled response.

My blood was boiling.

I launched at her across the table, grabbing her hair in one hand and throwing her head forwards, towards the table.

She squealed as her head struck the timber; loose strands of hair entangled between my fingers.

Three officers attempted to restrain me, as I screamed and cursed at her.

I know how people act in a situation is their karma, and how you react is yours. But I couldn't help myself.

Clumps of her black hair fell from my hands as I stumbled backwards.

'You're disgusting!' I said, pointing at her. 'Vijay doesn't love you. He's in lust. I give it a few months until he throws you away like the rest.'

Truth was, it was the way she'd spoken to me that had angered me most.

Had she sat there and told me she was in love with Vijay, I may have been understanding.

After all, our marriage was essentially over. I was numb to his affairs.

But the way she spoke was disrespectful. She was positive Vijay was going to leave me and marry her.

That's how we finished the conversation.

The police later went to charge me with assault but Vijay convinced them against it. After all, I couldn't easily return to Australia if I was charged with an offence in Fiji. And he would not be able to continue his relationship with Karun.

After flying home from Fiji, I resigned myself to the fact that Vijay was probably going to leave me. I started to find peace with that. I had a job as a massage therapist, and a home.

I also realised it was not the act of Vijay cheating that hurt me most, but of people finding out about it.

It was embarrassing.

Our relatives knew about his affairs but hadn't told me. No one wanted to hurt me. Afterwards, I wouldn't even sleep on my bed in Fiji as I knew he'd probably had another woman there.

In fact, from that day forward I never shared a bed with Vijay again. The marital bed, and Vijay, felt filthy to me.

When we returned to Australia, we found Vijay sitting in the front yard with a knife.

He wanted to scare us.

He informed me he was going to chop Neelma's legs off for challenging him and convincing me to go to Fiji.

It sounds completely absurd but he was all talk, no action.

I was never afraid of him.

I recognise now how wrong his actions were though.

I told him when he was ready to file for divorce, I was ready.

On October 30, 2002, we received a phone call from Tailevu in Fiji. The person told Vijay his wife and children would be murdered.

When I heard about the call, not even that scared me.

It's ludicrous to think it, but that was my life. I was used to the threats of violence, and a phone call from Fiji was the least of my worries.

It was these types of relationships, and threats, that police later investigated as part of the case. They needed to ensure no one in Fiji was involved in the deaths of our children.

CHAPTER 18

THE SHOWDOWN

In mid-November of 2002, Kunal graduated Year 12 and attended 'Schoolies' on the Gold Coast—a popular week-long celebration for school-leavers.

Sidhi also had an annual dance at her school—an island theme. She pinned a frangipani in her hair and wore a grass-coloured hula skirt with a tube top.

Not long after we had dropped her to the dance, Neelma told me something that no mother, or person, would ever want to hear.

'You know Papa has been touching Sidhi,' she said. 'In a bad way.'

'Who told you that, Nim?' I demanded. 'Who said such terrible things?'

'Max,' she said.

I was disgusted at what I was hearing but the truth was, I didn't really believe that Vijay would ever do that ... even if he was capable of hurting me.

When Sidhi's dance finished, and she arrived home, I asked her about Neelma's accusations. Sidhi told me it was Max who'd asked her if Vijay touched her.

She'd told him yes. But in Sidhi's words, 'Of course he does – he hugs me all the time!'

Max had manipulated those words. Even so, I decided to approach Vijay about the accusations. I downed several glasses of red wine, and at 1 am I climbed the stairs of our house and threw open the door of Sidhi's room, where Vijay was sleeping.

He often slept in Sidhi's room, while Sidhi slept with me in the main bedroom.

I grabbed Vijay by his T-shirt and shook him awake. I was raging, first about Karun, and secondly about Sidhi.

Vijay ran downstairs. I followed quickly, waving around a tin of hairspray as a weapon.

He'd locked himself in the office, at the front of our house. I threw the spray at the wall, screaming and bashing at the wooden door with my hands before searching for the spare key and letting myself in.

As the fight ensued, my eyes caught sight of a silhouette at our front door.

It was a person, a man.

I squinted, my eyes adjusting to the light.

It was Max.

I opened the door to let him in, not even stopping to consider why he was at our front door at that hour of the morning.

As Vijay struggled to close the office door, Max forced it open, pushing himself in, slamming the door behind him.

I paced back and forth banging on the door, the two of them now in the office alone.

The following is an excerpt from Vijay's Queensland Police Service Witness Statement from November 11, 2004.

'He rushed forward at me and took hold of my throat with his right hand. He also grabbed hold of my left wrist and pushed it back against my chest. He forced me backwards and held me up against the wall. I could feel pressure against my throat which was causing me pain.

He was yelling words to the effect of, "what did you do to your daughter, I'll fucking kill you, I'll fucking cave your head in. I'll fucking tear you apart."

He forced me down into a chair and held me down. He was holding my arms so that I could not get up.

He was right in my face yelling "sit down, I have fucking permission to be here, sit down, sit the fuck down."'

The police arrived a short time later.

I can only assume Neelma gave Max the heads-up that she'd told me about the rumours.

I was feisty and he knew I'd confront Vijay. He waited, in the dead of night, to swoop in as a protector when Vijay and I got into the fight.

He did everything possible to break our marriage—to weaken my bond with

Vijay and exert an influence over our family.

In the moment, I was glad he was there ... however, I always knew his behaviour was manipulative.

Vijay later left the house to live with Archana and Kavin.

And by the following month, Vijay's relationship with Karun was over.

His reasoning? She was bossy.

She later went to our house in Fjii to confront Vijay and threatened to kill herself with Paraquat weed killer.

I agreed this was a great idea and even offered to send her some from Australia.

In the meantime, Neelma continued to see Max on and off. In early 2003, Max told Neelma he had a brain tumour and that he had plans to commit suicide by driving off a mountain road. He said his parents were not aware of the tumour and that he only had six months to live.

He planned to take his life on March 23, 2003.

He told Neelma he would spend the day with his children and enjoy a barbecue before driving his dad's car off the side of Mount Nebo, a small township in the D'Aguilar Range, just outside of Brisbane.

Worried about him, Neelma spoke with Max for hours about the diagnosis, his kids, life and death.

However, I knew the story was a lie.

'He's trying to gain your attention and sympathy,' I told her. 'He's not dying.'

Kunal agreed.

'Neelma, we've got someone trying to kill themselves with weed killer in Fiji, and another dying with a brain tumour,' Kunal joked. 'What is our world coming to!'

I wanted Neelma to be happy, healthy, and safe, but Max compromised all three of those things. She was stuck in his vortex and I feared not even I could help her.

CHAPTER 19

THE EMAILS

The following is an extract from The Courier-Mail (Mark Oberhardt) on February 16, 2012.[19]

'The man accused of murdering the Singh siblings had earlier sent their father an anonymous email in which he hoped a Hindu god of destruction would 'put his hand' on him, a court heard yesterday. Investigating officer Joseph Zitny spent several hours introducing more than 100 photographs, diagrams, emails and tapes as exhibits into the trial yesterday.

The court heard Sica admitted sending emails from anonymous email addresses but not creating them all. The court heard Sica, using the name 'Peter Pan,' allegedly also sent naked photographs of Neelma Singh to a large number of people. Sica also sent emails to dozens of people in which he made allegations such as Vijay Singh was molesting his daughters. He concluded the email by saying: "May Shiva (a Hindu god of destruction) place his hand upon this man (Vijay)."'

On February 13, 2003, Vijay received an email on his business computer in Fiji from a 'Peter Pan.'

It was titled 'Vijay mama—baat' and spoke about a sexual liaison between Neelma and an employee of Vijay's company. In Hindi, baat means 'gossip'; a salacious subject like that was always going to be opened by many.

A second email on February 23, 2003, threatened Vijay and a third on March 6, 2003, contained naked photographic images of Neelma. The latter was sent to two of Vijay's business addresses, as well as relatives and members of the Fijian Indian community who shared a good relationship with our family.

I didn't receive the emails myself, but Vijay told me they showed Neelma on the toilet, and nude.[20]

I was devastated for Neelma, who blamed Max for their release.

'Mama, the one on the bed, fully naked, it's not me,' Neelma cried. 'I think it was a call girl Max spent time with.'

She was so ashamed. Her pride was hurt and she stayed in her room for two full days.

She also grew increasingly fearful of Max and was afraid to use her laptop, concerned he had bugged it.

At the time, Neelma and her ex-boyfriend Amit were growing closer again. She had even been invited to his brother's birthday party. Amit was angry about the photos though and refused to talk to her.

I was growing increasingly saddened by Max's effect on the children. His behaviour was manipulative and poisonous and, quite frankly, scary.

I decided to call him.

'Max … the email … it was nasty. You are a low-level person and you are ruining my daughter's life,' I spat down the phone. 'Our relatives from all over the world are so upset by what you've done to Neelma. They think you're sick.'

Truth was, the family was disgusted in Neelma as well. She had tarnished our Singh family name by revealing her body in such provocative poses. That type of behaviour was not accepted in our culture. But I wasn't going to admit that to him.

'I didn't do it,' he said.

'You did!' I screamed. 'I don't believe anything you say. You're a computer expert, no one else could take information from Neelma's computer—like the email addresses—except you. I am more mature and more bitter than she'll ever be in life,' I continued.

'Don't you dare think that anything you are doing is hurting us. Don't you dare think that you're driving a wedge between Neelma and her father, because you're not. You're only driving a wedge between *you* and Neelma.'

I later called Max's sister and parents to air my disgust and distrust of him. Of course, neither party was receptive.

Around the same time, other strange things started to happen around the house.

I found blinds retracted and doors unlocked.

Neelma also saw Max driving past the house and told me about a time he hid behind a public toilet on a vacant block near our house, watching. The stories were terrifying.

He was stalking her.

'Mum, I will only ever marry a person that you and Papa welcome with open arms,' Neelma assured me. 'Max is not that man. I'm done with him.'

My daughter was beautiful and intelligent. Max was controlling and manipulative. He was not worthy of her love. Naked pictures of our beautiful daughter were being distributed for all to see and our family was being repeatedly threatened. While everyone has skeletons in their closet, the Indian-Fijian community were an unforgiving bunch. People my daughter once respected were forwarding the emails further. They should have deleted them. It was disgusting.

Kunal got really angry as well, but not at Neelma. 'Don't worry, you're still my very pretty sister,' he told her. 'You'll find someone that you deserve, Neelma, someone that will respect you for the rest of your life.'

He hugged her, held her, and kissed her, assuring her everything would be okay.

Sidhi was too young to understand what was happening, however she seemed concerned.

'Max sent some horrible emails,' we told her.

'Well, horrible people do horrible things,' she reasoned. 'You'll be OK, Nim.'

It was such an innocent response by my beautiful Sidhi.

The kids had such a beautiful relationship. They loved each other so much.

Even still, we had a serious problem on our hands. We needed this man out of our lives.

CHAPTER 20

MY DREAMS

Not long after the kids passed away, they started to visit me in my dreams. I'd record every visit in my diaries as a way of keeping their spirits alive and savouring the memories.

Sidhi first visited me on the morning of May 28, 2003.

She came towards me, arms outstretched. She wanted a hug.

All I could think about was what she looked like when I'd identified her body. I asked her about the injuries to her head, and whether she was feeling okay.

'No, mum, I'm fine,' she commented, soothingly. She then told me Max had taken electrical cords from the cupboard downstairs and strangled Neelma.

I shook, my body convulsing as I woke.

While we'd not yet received the death certificates, I knew the children had been badly hurt, their bodies found in the spa bath. But we didn't know what implement had been used to kill them, or their official cause of death.

The police had questioned me about a garden fork found in the garage. I didn't think much of it.

I later told police about my dream of Sidhi.

Like Archana and Vijay, I was a suspect though. So, anything I said was up for questioning. At times it probably seemed like I knew more than I actually did.

Recalling my dreams to police became a regular occurrence from that point. They never formed part of the evidence but I'm sure they offered police with an insight to our family, our inner workings, and our love.

On another occasion I dreamt about my mother, washing the children's clothes in a river.

'What are you doing?' I asked. 'We have a washing machine at home.'

She laughed but didn't say anything. I asked her where the children were;

it was nearly night.

'It's dark, they need to come home before Vijay finds out,' I said.

I started to call out for Kunal, who I soon saw standing on a hill across the river, dressed like a priest. Priests typically wore orange or yellow, depending on their devotion. Kunal was wearing white. It was strange.

I yelled out for him to come home.

'No, mum, I can't. However, I'm here and I always will be.'

My cousin, the priest in Fiji, said this was a sign Kunal had crossed over to the other side, that he was in heaven.

'He's telling you he's with Lord Shiva,' he said.

I dreamt often, and vividly, about my children's beautiful faces, their dreams and ambitions, the good times and the bad. I'd talk to them, touch them, and cuddle them. It all felt very real, particularly in that first year. It never scared me when the children 'visited' me—it calmed me.

On one occasion Neelma stopped by.

'There's a creek, Mum, with a bridge going over it. Max has hidden the jewellery there,' she said. 'There's a blue plastic bag.'

I later told police, who asked which creek it was. But while I could see the river, and a large concrete bridge, I couldn't tell where it was.

On another evening I cried myself to sleep on our sofa upstairs. Next thing I opened my eyes and Sidhi was in front of me. She said nothing but turned around and shook her bum in my face.

I could not stop laughing. It cheered me up so much and reminded me about Sidhi's beautiful sense of humour. If I was angry, or if I screamed and yelled at her, she was always quick to try make me laugh, to lighten up the situation.

On another occasion, while I was crying, Kunal visited. I could feel his touch; my skin tingled, the hairs on my arm raised. 'Why are you crying?' he asked. 'I'm here, Mum, we all are. We aren't going to leave you.'

I wouldn't tell everyone about my dreams; I knew people would tell me I was crazy.

I wasn't making it up though. Every time they visited as heavenly angels, it was so vivid … so real.

To this day, they still visit, and every time I see them or talk to them, it's so special.

They always know the right time to drop in, the right thing to say.

CHAPTER 21

DIARIES

I first started keeping diaries when I started work as a massage therapist in Australia.

It was a good way to track the hours I was working, my expenses, and the clients I had.

I wrote about everything in my diaries.

Vijay and his affairs, the children, friends, family.

It was a great outlet for me. I found when I wrote stuff down, I got my feelings on the page and out of my system. I found it easier to express my feelings on paper instead of telling someone in person.

Neelma and Sidhi also kept diaries.

Neelma would write about her relationships, her time in Dubai.

She later started documenting her time with Max, their fights, and even the times Max would call her.

I never read the diary but I knew of its existence. Neelma had told me about it.

This diary went missing when the children were murdered.

Sidhi on the other hand would write about her friends' birthdays, going shopping, and saving money. Typical. She loved shopping, and always bought the best birthday presents.

After the children were murdered, my diaries became a way for me to express my thoughts about everything from Max to the police investigation, and my dreams.

They were my therapy, my outlet. That 'person' I could tell everything to.

In the early days after the children's murders, the police removed the diaries from my house as part of the investigation. I genuinely missed them when they were gone as I enjoyed re-reading the contents which were filled with memories. To others they may seem sad. But to me they were my truth; the life I'd lived. They were returned to me years later.

Edited excerpts from Shirley's diaries 2003–2004

May 14, 2003

Today was a day when I had to say goodbye to them. I wanted to kiss them and hold them, tell them their Lord is everywhere. No one can take the love or memories from me.

January 5, 2004

What shall I call this? Experience? Coincidence?

I woke this morning at 5:30 am. I was tossing and turning in my bed for a while. I finally got up and freshened. I turned on the CD and was listening to bhajans. I was crying to see my children, thinking about how I no longer have to get up early to make anyone's breakfast or lunch. Then, what happened? Neelma's photo fell near me. I had my eyes closed, crying. I sat up, shocked. How can it fall off the wall and land right next to me? I was so overwhelmed. I knew straight away she was telling me she is with me, and looking after me from heaven.

January 6, 2004

I want that pillow back, it's got my daughter's blood on it. I want to keep it. I regret not cutting a piece of Kunal's mattress or a piece of carpet from Nim's room.

February 9, 2004

I am angry. Kunal promised me lots of children. What is life without him? Or them? My son, my only son, was put to death in his room then in my spa. He might come out of the spa one day to come and tell me he still loves me.

February 10, 2004

How could anyone do such a cruel thing to my children? I can't understand why my children, of all people, had to experience such death and left the way they were. Where is justice? What is happening? Where is God and why is he taking so long? How am I going to spend the rest of my life?

March 4, 2004

My Sidhi's 13th birthday. Happy Birthday Sid! Hope you liked your gift. I had to buy you something similar to Nim's otherwise you will complain. You came forcefully into my life and were taken away from me too. Thank you for being there for me always. Thanks for the touch now and then. Thanks for telling me things. Baby, I miss you. Please tell God not to reincarnate you cause I want to be with you people just one more time. I want to do things for you. Wash, cook and clean. I have been cooking your favourite meals and feeding others. It makes me feel good. I know you enjoyed your party last year. This year, even though you are not present in body, I have invited a few of your friends over. Next year I will take your friends out. I will never stop marking your birthday because you were very special to me and always will be. Love you always, Mum xxx

CHAPTER 22

MEDIA

Media attention after the murders was fierce, and from the very early stages, journalists would camp out the front of our house waiting for developments in the case.

From April 23 to May 4, 2003, the story was covered in Brisbane's daily metropolitan newspaper, *The Courier-Mail*, every single day.

However, on May 5, there was nothing.

It was the same on May 6, May 7, May 8, May 9, and May 10.

While I knew police were busy on the case, it was days like these that really confused me. Were police still working to solve the murders? Had the public forgotten about us? Were the media sick of telling our story?

'There's nothing!' I'd yell, as Vijay and I took turns in searching the paper.

'It's all about the cupboard girl,' I protested, saddened.

Natasha Ryan, an 18-year-old girl missing and presumed murdered since 1998, had been found alive and well in a cupboard of her boyfriend's house during a raid of a North Rockhampton property in Central Queensland on April 10.

She quickly became known as 'the girl in the cupboard' and her story had captured the nation's attention.

In a way, I actually looked forward to reading the newspaper each day.

It reminded me of my beautiful children, the love their school friends had for them, and the hard work of the police investigators working on the case in those first few weeks.

May 11 was Mother's Day, my first without three of my children.

Again, we were on the front page of the state's metropolitan weekend newspaper, *The Sunday Mail*.

Dad's Brave Walk, it read, with a photo of Vijay and Archana entering our Grass Tree Close home. A day earlier, police had removed the crime-scene tape for the first time.

Despite the constant surveillance, the media always treated us fairly, and with respect. As the sun beat down on them, I would offer them water and food: curries, roti, and rice.

I was always looking for clues to assist police in their inquiries, and even called them after seeing an advertisement for the television show *CSI: Crime Scene Investigation*, where a person was murdered during a visit to a spa.

Turns out Max was also a fan of CSI, and it was an angle police would later follow up.

I became quite obsessed with crime shows during this time, and still watch many of them today: 'CSI', 'NCIS', 'Criminal Minds', 'Victims of Homicide', and 'Law and Order: Special Victims Unit.'

The following is an excerpt from the Australian Associated Press, June 27, 2003.

'Police investigating the brutal murders of three Brisbane siblings are viewing tapes of the American television show "CSI" for clues.

A Channel Nine Queensland spokeswoman confirmed today police investigating the murders of Neelma, Kunal and Sidhi Singh had asked to see episodes of the popular crime show.

But she refused to comment further because of the "ongoing nature of the criminal investigation."

Police were also tight-lipped about the case today, refusing to comment on why they'd asked to see tapes of the show, a police drama that deals with forensic investigations of murders and other crimes.

The bodies of Neelma, 24, Kunal, 18, and 12-year-old Sidhi were found in their upmarket Bridgeman Downs home, on Brisbane's northside, on April 22. They were dumped in a hot spa bath, making it difficult for police to pinpoint an exact time of death.'

In the early stages, Max was also engaging the media regularly.

In my opinion he was on a mission to taint the Singh name and would tell them stories about Vijay's affairs and his relationship with Neelma.

The Indian community believed many of his lies and would question me in the street, or the shopping centre, about Neelma's relationship.

'But why was she sleeping with that man, out of marriage?' they would ask. It upset me a lot. I'd tell them to mind their own business.

In an interview with 'A Current Affair' in mid-2003, Max made a number of claims to journalist David Margan. These included that he'd slept with Neelma six out of the seven days leading up to her death and that they were engaged to marry. He also spoke about finding the children's bodies, shared text messages between him and Neelma, and showed the journalist a lock of Neelma's hair and a wrapper from a lolly she'd once eaten.

His father, Carlo, was even quoted at the time saying, 'If I would imagine Max would be able to do something like that, police wouldn't need to worry about him, I would kill him with my bare hands.'

Put your words before your mouth, I thought. Save police the money and strangle him yourself.

However, it wasn't just the murder case receiving attention during this time. Max's background was also in the spotlight.

On July 13, 2003, *The Courier-Mail* wrote of Max's lifelong ambition to be a police officer.

According to a report tendered by psychologist Tony Robinson during sentencing for the 83 offences in 1993, Max had an ambition to be a police officer, which he'd garnered from an early age.

'He claimed that on one occasion he had been annoyed that "the police were not doing their job" when there was no response to an alarm which he had set off when committing an offence.

'It would seem then that his contact with the police following his offences could be traced back to his frustrated desire to be a police officer himself and, in an irrational way, he was expressing anger at the police at the same time "proving" that he was "smarter" and more competent than them.'

In his report, Mr Robinson said Max had difficulty controlling impulses, exhibited marked self-centredness and grandiosity, and was a sensation-seeker.

Psychiatrist Dr Ian Curtis later wrote that Max was a 'disturbed individual' with 'ongoing difficulties with his inner controls and with social limits.'

'This man suffers from an immature, dramatic personality with a major feature being gross immaturity and high impulsivity, with antisocial features,' he said.

A week later, the same publication reported Max was suing the Queensland Government for more than $500,000 in damages for personal injuries allegedly suffered as a prisoner at Numinbah Correctional Centre, south of Brisbane.

Back pain, he claimed.

Sure as hell didn't look like he had any back pain when I knew him.

Disgustingly, after Max was sentenced to jail in 2012, his second wife, Shiv—with whom he had one daughter, Nakiesha, and married in 2008—was allegedly paid $50,000 to do an interview with 'A Current Affair'. The story raised a potential 'other killer' and questioned evidence tendered in court. The Queensland Homicide Victims' Support Group slammed both the payment and the story.

'A Current Affair' bureau chief Amanda Paterson said no money had been paid directly to the Sica family but refused to comment on whether a Brisbane public relations agency acting on Shiv's behalf had been paid.

'For the record, ACA has not paid Shiv Sica or the Sica family one cent,' Paterson said.[21]

CHAPTER 23

THE POLICE

'While Vijay and Shirley were very literate, articulate and spoke well ... they didn't always understand what we were saying. They would often confuse something I was asking for something else. Sometimes I'd have to re-say something two or three times, to ensure they understood. When he was with us, Arveen assisted us in bridging that gap.'

—**Bryan Paton**

From the very start of the investigation into our children's murders, we were frustrated.

The police would only tell us superficial stories, nothing in-depth. They'd advise us the case was progressing, but they wouldn't tell us anything more. We understood it was very important no information was leaked but it was still frustrating.

We wanted the person, or people, who had murdered our children to be caught.

We had great respect for the police working on our case—in particular Detective Senior Sergeant Bryan Paton, Detective Sergeant Joe Zitny, Detective Sergeant Andrew Massingham, Detective Senior Constable Kurt Naumann, Senior Constable Arveen Singh, and Sergeant Ritchie Callaghan.

Joe Zitny and Kurt Naumann were the arrest team and Bryan was in charge of the investigation for the North Brisbane Region. Joe then led the case when Bryan left the force.

While there were plenty of very serious and tough moments, there were also some lighter times.

On my first birthday after the children were murdered, I was interviewing with police at Petrie. We finished at 3 am the morning of my 52nd birthday.

A million thoughts swirled through my head.

Who's going to wake me up in the morning? Who's going to wish me happy birthday? Who's going to cook me breakfast?

I asked Detective Sergeant Zitny for a cuddle, and he obliged, holding onto me tightly, just like my children always would.

As Vijay and I were both suspects, I really appreciated it.

Needless to say, that birthday was the worst I'd ever experienced but that hug meant the world to me.

On another occasion, police asked if Kunal had cannabis in his room.

'Yes, he's got heaps,' I responded. 'I used to buy it for him. I mean, I didn't pick it for him, but I'd give him the money to buy it.'

The police looked concerned.

'Here, I'll show you!' I exclaimed, as I took off up the stairs and into Kunal's room. I flung open his cupboard and gestured at the floor.

'See! Canvas shoes! Lots of them.'

The police looked perplexed.

'No, Shirley, cannabis. CANN-A-BIS. You know, marijuana. Weed?'

'Ohhh, no way!' I exclaimed. 'Definitely no cannabis here. Only canvas.'

The police could not stop laughing.

And nor could I. My bloody accent often got me into trouble!

Luckily Arveen was a great help in situations like this. He ensured them Kunal didn't have marijuana in his room, but was in fact the owner of four or five pairs of canvas shoes.

When I visited the police at the station, I noticed they weren't eating or drinking. 'You're doing such a marvellous job,' I'd say. 'But you don't ever eat or drink. That's weird!'

'There's work to do, Shirley,' they'd respond.

The first time I did my written statement in 2005 was the first time I cooked for them. They absolutely loved the food and with time, midday feasting became a regular occurrence.

I'd take them curries and rice; butter chicken was their favourite. Bryan decided he loved Indian so much that he wanted to take his wife to a local Indian restaurant. When the restaurant asked if he wanted his food mild or hot, he asked for hot.

Needless to say, he was slightly regretful. His forehead was peppered with sweat and his mouth burned.

I laughed at him later. 'You never order hot food at an Indian restaurant! Indian hot is different to Australian hot!'

I'd also go for briefings at the Queensland Police Service Headquarters in Brisbane City. I would always make sure there was plenty of food for everyone to eat.

My humour often got me into trouble with the police too.

After repeated attempts by a journalist to meet me for coffee, I told police I wasn't keen. It felt like a date.

'I only sleep with Jacob,' I said. 'He's the only one that gives me peace and helps put me to sleep. In fact, people bring him over for me!'

The police stared at me, mouths open, in shock.

After exploring hundreds of lines of inquiry in the investigation, including Vijay's affairs, the swingers' clubs, massage clients and prank calls, not one person had ever mentioned Jacob to them.

'Shirley, why are we only hearing about Jacob now? You've never mentioned another man, nor has anyone else.'

I opened the bar fridge, holding a bottle of Jacob's Creek Merlot high in the air.

'Here he is,' I laughed. 'Best man ever. Smooth, doesn't talk back. Helps with relaxation.'

Detective Senior Sergeant Bryan Paton put his hands on his hips, frowning.

'Shirley Singh, be careful what you say to us!'

CHAPTER 24

THE SUPPORT

'Students at St Anthony's at Kedron had Sidhi's name included on the school's traditional Year 7 shirt, even though she died in Year 6.

Her best friend, Priyanka Senaratna, then 11, said she missed 'everything' about Sidhi.

Principal John Leyden said the school celebrated Sidhi's birthday on March 4 but would not mark the anniversary of her death.

The pupils received their shirts on a school camp.'

—In 'Memories of Sidhi' by Rebecca Galton, Northside Chronicle, April 21, 2004

The children's former schools, friends, and family were such a great support. It says a lot for the importance of having people around when you've gone through a period of grief. Every phone call, every meal dropped around, every bunch of flowers, and every conversation meant so much.

Some were genuine with their assistance; others were less genuine, stickybeaks who just wanted to know the gossip.

Some would cook us food, others would buy flowers, and others would simply just offer to help.

Interestingly, the Sicas never once gave us a phone call or sent a card or flowers in those early days.

Our front yard was full of flowers from acquaintances, neighbours, and strangers grieving the tragedy.

To me, the Sicas' lack of contact was significant.

Family travelled from all around the world to be with us, including loved ones from New Zealand, the US, and Fiji.

Given what we were going through, the support from those closest to us was welcomed.

They were the ones that knew us best. They were the ones that kept me strong, that talked sense into me when I drank too much wine, and that convinced me chemicals could not heal my pain, in relation to the antidepressants I was taking.

My friend Angie Power was also such an amazing pillar of support. She came into my life not long after the murders.

Angie had her own family—a husband, Chris, and three beautiful children, Adam, Mark, and Brianna—but she spent so much time looking after me in those early days.

On some nights I would leave the house doors and windows open and sit on the front steps with a knife, waiting for the murderer to come home.

Angie would take the knife off me, close my windows and doors, and help me to bed. She would look after me in shifts, with the police returning to see me just as Angie would leave again.

Sometimes she would call the house to make sure I didn't answer … just to make sure I was asleep.

When I answered, she'd drive over and help soothe me to sleep.

Angie never had the honour of meeting my children in life. Her knowledge of them is through my eyes. To this day though, she always knows the right things to say and the best memory to re-live.

The parents of other students, and the children's friends, were also so helpful and kind. They'd make food and biscuits and send messages and cards. This continued for weeks and months after the children's deaths. It would always make me smile and remind me of how popular the children were, how many people our story had impacted, and how their memory would live on in people's hearts for many years to come.

I know it's hard to know what to do or say when someone is grieving, but I know what felt good to us.

I appreciated those that offered their support, or asked how we were.

Those that listened to what I had to say and showed compassion.

Those that reserved their judgement on our situation and allowed me to open up.

And those that gave me silence when I needed it.

CHAPTER 25

LOSING MY MIND

'On one occasion, we found her in the spa bath. She'd tried to drown herself. She became aggressive when police tried to help her out. Everyone was mortified, in tears. They had to restrain her and take her to the mental hospital. I visited her so many times in the hospital and it broke my heart every time as she'd be such a despairing character the next day as she come down from the haze of alcohol and drugs.'
—**Bryan Paton**

Each day I woke, I'd reflect on the possibility I was a day closer to the murderer being caught.

While this gave me some comfort, along with the memories of Nim, Kunal, and Sid, it was the only light I had in my very dark world.

Vijay and I were barely on speaking terms and our finances left little to be desired. Stress started to plague much of my waking moments.

On February 17, 2004, I decided to drown those emotions the only way I knew how; with merlot.

I drank two bottles of wine and a handful of Stilnox, and phoned police.

'Let me speak to the police commissioner,' I demanded. 'If you don't let me speak to him, I will set fire to the house and burn myself.'

The person I was requesting was Bob Atkinson, Commissioner of the Queensland Police Service from 2000 until 2012. I was still on the phone to the Queensland Police when ambulance, fire, and police swarmed our street. I pushed and clawed at the paramedics as they tried to sedate me.

'I don't want to be here anymore!' I screamed. 'Leave me alone. I'm done. I want to go.'

That is my last memory of that night.

* * *

According to hospital records, I was transported to the Mental Health Service at The Prince Charles Hospital on February 18, 2004, by seven police officers. I was intoxicated, angry, hostile, distressed, and agitated. I smelled strongly of alcohol, was uncooperative, and walked out on my admission interview.

I would remain in the hospital for the next eight days.

It was my third admission to the hospital in six months.

Relationship strain, alcohol, and benzodiazepine use were all noted on my admission records.

I knew the drugs and alcohol were no good for me but I wanted the pain to go away. Both dulled the ache I felt inside.

Following my discharge from the hospital on February 26, 2004, I was still having trouble sleeping. And so, a few nights later I drank red wine again.

One glass, then another.

Two bottles in, I passed out.

I woke to the feeling of a presence in the room.

It was Kunal.

'Mum, don't do this to yourself. Wine is not good for you. It hurts to see you this way,' he said.

Did Kunal just visit me to tell me to stop drinking?

I later told the officers: 'I'm not having any more red wine!'

It was a sentence I uttered many times in those days but one I rarely stuck to.

On March 6, 2004, I woke ready to celebrate Sidhi's 13th birthday with her friends. We prepared chicken curry, potato, and roti and readied the house for a small party. We listened to music, shared food, and told stories of our beautiful Sidhi.

However, as the party ended, I felt lost and alone.

I ended up in hospital the next day, unable to recollect details of the night before, 'depressed, fidgety and judgement impaired.'

I knew I needed to be strong but I was grieving.

On Kunal's 19th birthday in August 2004, I set up a shrine in our front yard. Around 15 of his friends joined us for a celebration of his life. Archana bought a model-sized Nissan Skyline for Kunal, which we placed in the shrine and later moved to his room. I made his favourite chicken curry and chutney and we sat around sharing stories about my beautiful boy.

After Kunal's friends left, I had a glass of merlot. Archana and Kavin helped clean up and told me to go for a shower.

As I climbed the stairs, the phone rang.

It was my son Janel. He told me his wife was pregnant; that the family would soon welcome a new baby to replace Kunal.

I know he meant well, that he was trying to make me happy with news of a new grandchild ... but it was not the right wording.

I got angry.

'How dare you say that to me! Nobody can replace Kunal,' I screamed, slamming the phone down.

I flung myself onto Kunal's bed and cried. Deep stomach-wailing cries. I felt suffocated and I dry-retched as my body heaved, tears rolling down my cheeks.

I didn't want to stay in this sinful world, full of evil people. I wanted to join Kunal, Neelma, and Sidhi in heaven, I decided.

I started dropping Stilnox, one after the other, until I got to six.

I filled the same bath my children were found in with hot water, and got in.

Archana, who knew I was usually quick to shower, soon came looking for me.

She found me in the bath, breathing but non-responsive.

She dialled 000 and I was transported to The Prince Charles Hospital, where I was again admitted to the mental health ward.

When I woke up, I was upset I was still alive. Then I got upset that I was stuck in the hospital and not at home with my children.

I was placed on antidepressants and started counselling.

I stayed in the hospital 13 nights on that occasion, the longest of any of my visits.

Afterwards my brother Jayant told me to not take the antidepressants.

'You need to keep a focused mind for court. You need to help police catch the killer,' he said.

While I was able to stop the medication, dropping the alcohol was harder.

When I couldn't sleep, the drinking helped.

On some nights I'd sit for hours on my balcony, praying the killer would return.

I'd watch my reflection bounce from bottle to glass under the haze of the moonlight.

On other occasions, I'd stop drinking and make the kids food for their school lunches. I'd also cook them breakfast—eggs and toast—and place them on the table for them to eat.

I'd boil a kettle of tea for the table and place two cups at Kunal's place. He always dipped his bread in the tea of one cup, while drinking from the other.

It felt normal to make their food.

Some nights I'd down wine and Stilnox and walk to the cemetery in my night gown to look for Sidhi.

I wasn't in the right state of mind to be going anywhere but I had no focus and I wasn't thinking properly. Stumbling drunk, I'd weave haphazardly through my estate towards the cemetery; a 30-minute walk. When I got there, I would hold onto the gates and peer through the bars for hours. Hoping and waiting for the children to walk towards me.

Sometimes I'd pass out there. As the morning light pierced the sky, I'd wake at the base of the gate, pick myself up and walk home.

Officers later visited me for a 'chat.'

'We need you, Shirley, we need you to be fit and healthy and strong,' they said. 'You are a prime witness and you know everything we need. If you hurt yourself, we won't be able to catch the person or persons responsible.'

They showed me a picture of the prison and asked me if I wanted the person responsible to be locked up in there.

I agreed.

It started to sink in.

If I harm myself, the killer wins.

Around two years after the children were murdered, I met Bruce and Denise Morcombe at a Queensland Homicide Victims' Support Group meeting in Brisbane. Their son Daniel had been abducted from the Sunshine Coast on December 7, 2003, on his way to a local shopping centre. He was only 13.[22]

On this day, I remember seeing Denise shaking. I asked her if she was taking antidepressants. She nodded. I told her not to take them, to keep a clean mind … just like I'd been told.

'It's important you stay strong, have clarity,' I said. 'It's important for getting justice.'

On March 13, 2014, convicted paedophile Brett Peter Cowan was sentenced to life in prison for Daniel's murder.

CHAPTER 26

SAVOURING MEMORIES

Each time I returned from the hospital I'd try and get on with my life.

I felt empty though. I felt lost.

I stopped doing all the things I'd once loved.

I didn't attend parties or weddings. I stopped cutting my hair and doing my make-up. I even stopped shopping for groceries, as the grocery store reminded me of them.

Kunal would push the trolley as we walked the aisles. On one particular day, he ran off through the shops with my handbag. He thought he was hilarious. I had to get staff to page him over the loudspeaker.

'Kunal Singh—if you are in the shopping centre, can you please come to customer service with your mother's handbag. She needs to pay for your food.'

Sidhi loved chocolate milk and Kinder Surprise and Kunal loved Coca-Cola. They both loved multi-pack chips.

Because of this, I couldn't stand visiting the aisles with Coke, chips, or juice and still find it hard today. If I'm having a bad day, I skip those aisles, I don't even stop.

Believe it or not, I still have a half drunk can of Coke in my fridge from Kunal, and one of Sidhi's flavoured milks. They sit in prime position in the fridge; top shelf. I connect memories of their favourite things to happy times together and it makes me feel good.

On each of their first birthdays after they died, I was angry. However, as the years went on, I started to celebrate their birthdays. I'd cook their favourite meals, buy them cake and presents, as well as their favourite groceries. They may not have been here physically, but I soon realised there was no point upsetting myself when I should be celebrating their memory.

It would give me something to look forward to.

When I started celebrating the children's birthdays most people thought I was crazy, but my close family understood. We placed photos of the children around the house, and as we'd cook, we'd talk to them. Nim hated pumpkin curry and we'd apologise profusely as its smell wafted through the house.

To us, this was our coping mechanism.

Their bodies had been physically taken but their memories hadn't.

Having their smiling faces on the wall blocked out those terrible images: of the crime scene, identifying their bodies, and seeing their caskets.

In the early stages following their deaths, I was told the jury may one day have to visit the house. I knew it was important I still lived there, and that it was in its closest form to how it was when they were killed. I also didn't want to leave the house when my children's murderer hadn't been caught.

* * *

In the years following their deaths, I had lots of calls from psychics. I never wanted to speak to them though. Many knew of my story and I feared they'd tell me what I wanted to hear.

One time a lady from the Gold Coast called. She claimed to be a psychic, and that she was convinced Max was the murderer.

It turned out she was a friend of Max's looking to see how I would react. When I realised who she was, I was so angry. I might have been grieving but I wasn't stupid!

A few years after the murders I saw a psychic, a Hawaiian man, on Brisbane's northside.

I wanted to feel connected to the children and to know they were OK so I thought he could help me.

As I sat in front of him, he held my hand. He told me he saw an aeroplane and a flight attendant. He mentioned a 12-year-old girl sitting on my lap, with a boy standing behind me.

He acknowledged the number three, that my heart was bleeding and that I was in pain.

He then started crying. He told me he couldn't read me anymore, that it was too much.

He got up and walked away. He didn't even charge me!

I was also contacted regularly by mothers from around Australia in those first few years. They'd write me letters, tell me they empathised with what I was going through, and to remain strong. They'd also send me flowers and Mother's Day cards.

In the first four or five years, our porch would be filled with flowers on Mother's Day. From neighbours, the media, and people who had followed our story. It was comforting to be sent such beautiful gifts; it reminded us people were thinking of us.

I would also spend my days watching mythological DVDs like 'Om Namah Shivay' and 'Krishna'. It would help give me strength, calm me, and take my focus away from grieving for a while.

It moved me away from the dirty thoughts, the bad memories, and the frustration.

To this day, I still watch them.

CHAPTER 27

THE INVESTIGATION HEATS UP

'I always maintained my objectivity when it came to Max's guilt. Max was the prime witness from the start as he found the bodies. As things progressed in the case, and we investigated all avenues, the door kept swinging back towards him. I particularly felt Max was guilty, after his 18-hour interview. I remember we had the fork in the interview room and he absolutely freaked when he saw it, he went white.'

—**Bryan Paton**

On March 31, 2004, the investigation into the murders ramped up.

During a visit to the parole board, Max was summoned by police. He underwent 18 hours of interrogation, returning home at dawn.

The police later removed items from his house including stuffed toys, a baseball bat, a rifle, and videotapes.

Max's father, Carlo, was very critical of the interrogation, telling Channel 9 journalist Steve Marshall the items should have been removed from the house 12 months prior.

The Sica family also reported media had arrived at their house up to 30 minutes before police, backing their ongoing allegations that the police were closely intertwined with media in the case.

Investigators defended the operation, saying the interrogation was voluntary. Police later said the raids had moved the investigation forward, and that they hoped to have a conclusion to the case 'soon.'

Of course, for us, 'soon' could not come quick enough.

On April 6, 2004, search warrants were executed on Max's sisters' homes at Enoggera and Everton Hills. Police removed a number of items, including clothing. They even X-rayed the walls of the Sicas' family home at Stafford Heights and admitted publicly for the first time that Max was 'the main person of interest to our investigation.'

At the time, Max was represented by the firm of civil liberties campaigner Terry O'Gorman, who said he was furious his client had been detained without any legal representation. Terry accused the police of 'trial by media' and lodged a complaint with the Crime and Misconduct Commission about police leaks to reporters.

Max underwent four hours of forensic testing led by a specialist who worked on the infamous Snowtown murderers; a series of homicides committed by John Bunting, Robert Wagner and James Vlassakis between August 1992 and May 1999 in South Australia.[23]

Investigators had also found the imprint of a sock-covered foot, soaked in bleach, on one of our stairs. So, as part of the testing, police took an imprint of Max's foot. They then built a database of some 10,000 footprints, including mine, Vijay's, and Archana's.

A Canadian Forensic Expert who specialised in foot impressions was flown to Australia and Max was asked to replicate his movements up a makeshift staircase, which had been built at Petrie Police Station. It was identical to the one in our home built by Henley Homes, with the same timber, underlay, and carpet.

This part of the investigation would later prove to be a crucial element in the case against Max.

On April 25, 2004, we marked a year since the children were taken.

It was a painful time that brought back many memories of the sick, insane, evil, and cowardly person or persons that had taken their lives.

Surrounded by 100 family and friends, and members of the Fijian Indian community, Vijay, Archana, and I lit candles in New Farm Park at dusk, while family and friends spoke about their love for my three beautiful children.

The park—one of Brisbane's oldest, grandest and largest—was a place we'd spent much family time over the years, a spot very special to us.

Kunal's former school principal even spoke, announcing the inauguration of the Kunal Singh Cup for the best and fairest player in the intra-school soccer competition.

It was a fantastic tribute to a boy that loved his soccer so much.

While I tried hard to be a pillar of strength for Archana and support my children's friends, behind the scenes I was starting to break.

After 18 months—547 days—of last seeing my children alive, I met with the Queensland Police for an update on the investigation.

I pleaded with them for answers.

'How long will we have to wait; how long will this take?' I asked.

The police said they were completing a brief of evidence, already 15,000 pages in length.

'We've had ten detectives working on the case full time, Shirley,' they said.

My mum and dad (my adopted parents) Ram and Gayatri Dutta when they were 40 years old and 38 years old respectively. My dad died two years later.

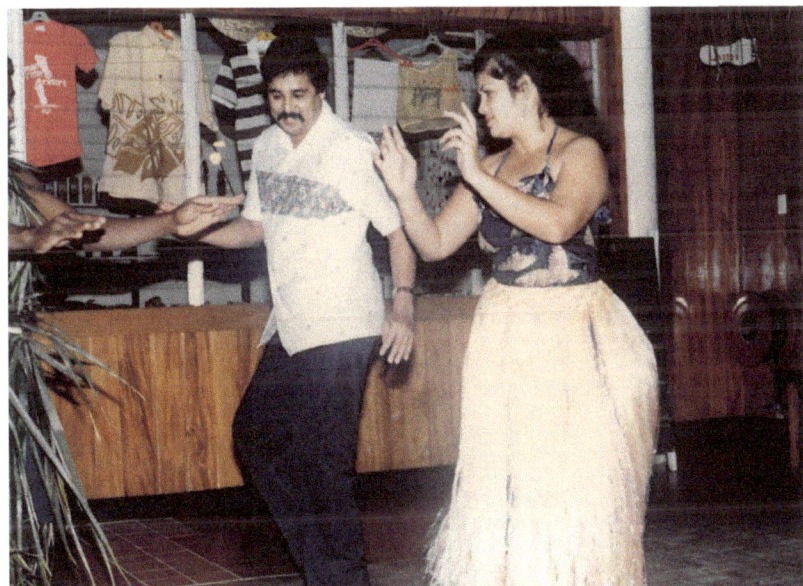

At one of Vijay's staff parties in 1985 at Man Friday Resort in Fiji. I loved to dance and would hula regularly, a very common dance in Fiji.

At our new house in Stafford Heights, just after we moved to Australia, 1993.

The kids first day at their new Australian schools: Kunal at St James College, Spring Hill and the girls at Corpus Christie College, Nundah, 1994.

The kids loved cartoons; Bugs Bunny was a favourite character. Kunal and Sidhi, 1994.

My kids were always dressed to the nines.

Enjoying a professional family photoshoot. I'm pictured with (L-R) Neelma, Sidhi, Vijay, Archana and Kunal, 1994.

Enjoying dinner at South Bank with my brother, Ashok, in 1995. He visited from Canada. He's pictured with Sidhi, Archana, Kunal and Neelma.

Kunal and Sidhi getting ready for Christmas at our Stafford Heights home in 1996.

During a trip to Singapore in 1997. We spent much of our time shopping for outfits for Archana's wedding.

Neelma, Kunal, Sidhi and Archana at our Stafford home during the Hindu festival for Raksha Bandhan in 1997, which celebrates the relationship of brother-sister. This is one of my favourite photos, ever. This photo was used widely by the media.

Archana's graduation from IT at university. We were so proud of her, 1997.

My beautiful girls celebrating the first Diwali after Archana's wedding in 1998. Diwali Festival of Lights celebrates the victory of light over darkness, good over evil, and knowledge over ignorance.

Sidhi, Kunal and Neelma were always very close. This was them on Sidhi's 8th birthday in 1998 at Archana's house. When the children died, I slept with this photo almost every night. It's so crumpled but so special to me.

At Neelma's 21st birthday, 1999. We celebrated with a party for 180 people at a local Italian club.

A colourful family picture, from Archana's sister-in-law's wedding. Vijay actually wasn't there. We photoshopped him in later, 2002.

With my best friend Angie Power, 2021.

Kunal's friends from high school came over for dinner at our Bridgeman Downs home. It was great to catch up with them after so many years, 2022.

CHAPTER 28

THE LOST YEARS

Days, weeks, and months passed. Then years.

Did I lose hope the case would ever be closed? Sure.

But I knew the police were working hard. I had faith justice would be served; I just knew we had to be patient.

At times Vijay and I doubted ourselves and our faith. While we were no longer together as partners, we were together in life to catch the person or persons who'd taken our children. No matter what had happened previously, Vijay had also lost his children and he was hurting.

The pain of dealing with the crime made us untrusting and reluctant to deal with the outside world. I spent most of my days celebrating the memory of our children, and spending time with friends and family.

I focused my attention on knowing that one day soon, the murderer would be charged.

Archana and Kavin moved to Melbourne and while she would sometimes call, our relationship was strained.

On a visit two or three years after the children were murdered, Kavin picked me up from the bus station and we returned to their two-bedroom unit in Gardenvale, maybe 20 minutes by car from Melbourne city.

I sat in their unit, waiting for Archana to return. She was out drinking with friends and walked in the door at 2 am. I was so excited to see her. However, I was bothered.

Why had she not been there to greet me?

Did she not miss me?

'You knew I was coming, why weren't you home?' I later questioned.

I knew she was upset and that I was a reminder of what had happened.

It's why she'd moved away from Brisbane; why she withdrew. But it hurt.

At our home, I set up shrines. In the living room and in the spa.

I put photos of the children through the house; birthdays, weddings, Christmas and Easter. In them the children were smiling, happy, and together.

I'd sit for hours staring at a painting Kunal gave me—it was of three rocks sitting in an ocean.

In the image, water hit the rocks with force, their turquoise hues splitting into whitewash and foam under a clear blue sky. It represented a story my mother had once told me, when I was going through a terrible time with Vijay.

'Enjoy your life,' mum had said. 'You and the children don't deserve any less than a life filled with fun and laughter. Pretend you're a rock in the middle of the ocean; a rock being hit by waves that never budges. Only then shall you feel the strength to keep moving forward. To realise how strong you really are.'

Each night I'd kiss pictures of the children before tucking the photos into their beds.

I still do this, 20 years on.

The police continued to work hard behind the scenes. They tapped phone lines, completed additional forensic and DNA testing, and interviewed clients and former business associates of all suspects.

They reinterviewed the tradesmen who'd witnessed Max enter our house on April 22, 2003, in addition to another 750 different witnesses.

Separate to our case, Max was also charged with 21 sex offences in 2008, including two counts of rape and one count of maintaining a sexual relationship with a child. He also faced nine counts each of unlawful carnal knowledge and indecent dealings of a child under 16. The alleged offences happened from November 2004 to September 2008.[24]

However, a judge later found him not guilty on all counts and he was acquitted.[25]

It was yet another chapter in the murky world of Max Sica.

I couldn't wait for him to be caught; we just knew it was a matter of time.

CHAPTER 29

THE CAPTURE

The following was the front page of The Courier-Mail newspaper (Michael Wray, Jodie Munro-O'Brien and Alex Dickinson) on December 31, 2008:

'CHARGED: After more than five and a half years, and one of the most complex investigations in Queensland police history, the man who once publicly announced he was the prime suspect in the deaths of the three Singh siblings has been accused of their murder. Max Sica and his new wife of just eight days were preparing to head to Noosa for their honeymoon when homicide detectives arrived on his doorstep north of Brisbane early yesterday.'

On December 30, 2008, my cousin from India, Shiromani (who has since sadly passed away), was visiting.

Shiromani and I grew up together and had always been very close. She was a loving and caring person, with an amazing sense of humour and impeccable dress sense.

It had been Neelma's 30th birthday the day before, and we'd been up all night talking. We went to bed at maybe 1:30 am.

I woke as soon as the sun rose and the first rays of light hit my bed through the drapes, which I drew together before bed. I covered my eyes with an eye mask, just like I did every morning. But I couldn't sleep.

Suddenly I heard a knock.

I looked out of our sliding door and saw a car.

I was still in my pyjamas, my hair a mess and my teeth unbrushed.

However, this was a car familiar to me and not even unkempt hair or morning breath was going to stop me from getting to it.

I flew down the stairs and threw open the door.

In front of me stood Assistant Commissioner Mike Condon and another officer.

'Have you arrested him?' I asked.

'Yes, Shirley. We've arrested Max Sica. He's been taken to police headquarters.'

I probably wasn't thinking straight but I bent down to touch his feet. In India, that signified respect and gratefulness. I was actually completely numb. I thanked him profusely and hugged him.

Then I excused myself to freshen up.

Vijay and my cousin soon woke up. Just like me, they were ecstatic with the news. It was like a celebration.

I always knew Max would be caught; it was just a matter of time.

For me, this was my aha moment. *We caught you, you asshole!*

And I was loving it.

Only eight days prior, Max had exchanged vows with his second wife, Shiv, at the St Francis of Assisi Parish Church in Nundah.

He was packing his bags for his honeymoon when police knocked on his door.

He'd actually told the media, not long before he was arrested, that he was marrying the love of his life, then going on a long holiday.

I think the 'long holiday' was prison—I think he knew his time was up.

Within hours, Max's arrest was leaked to the media and our street was swarming with reporters. It was at this time Acting Assistant Commissioner Condon advised me to no longer speak to the media.

'Tell the journalists to leave you alone, you can no longer speak to them. Anything you say could affect the case and we don't want that. Oh … and Shirley, please don't feed them anymore,' he said.

He didn't want me to do anything that would jeopardise the case, and I appreciated that.

When the police left my house, I cried.

For years Vijay and I had fought like cats and dogs. In ways, we had blamed each other for what had happened.

Vijay would say he was only in Fiji to earn money for me and the kids, and that I had let Max in the house repeatedly, allowing the relationship between

Max and Neelma to blossom.

I would tell him it was his fault because he'd had ongoing affairs. I'd say it was payback; karma.

The truth was, though, no matter what we did, it wouldn't have stopped our children from being murdered.

We loved them more than anything. No matter how bad the stories that came out in the press, no matter how bad the truth was, Vijay and I always stuck together. We wanted justice for our children, and we wanted to walk that road together.

This was just the start.

No one gets away from the law and the Lord.

'In terms of the time and effort we had to go to in order to solve the murders, Max almost committed the 'perfect crime.' There were classic indicators he couldn't change though, and that was the dynamics between him and the victims and the victimology in and around the way in which the offence was committed. You have to ask yourself, who else? Close up manual strangulation, a person that doesn't want the relationship to end and one that does, conflict. Strangulation was often indicative of domestic homicide incidents. This was a man that was also due to attend the property that night. The bleach bottle had Neelma's blood on it. If you identified the footprint, you identified the killer. It tied to the method that was used to cover the tracks of the killer. The use of bleach very quickly to a crime scene was clever. He had learned that from his previous experience in jails. He had those machinations, if you like. Once he'd committed the crime in that house, he was very quickly able to go into clean-up mode. We never referred to Max as the prime suspect—that was a tag he gave himself. We were always looking at other lines of investigation. We had more than 50 people we actively looked at, as a suspect.'

—Andrew Massingham

CHAPTER 30

TIME FOR JUSTICE

On August 13, 2009, I woke ready to get justice for my children. It was the first day of Max's committal hearing.

Max's family arrived wearing bright green T-shirts with the words 'Now the real truth about the Singhs will be known.' On the back they read, 'The guilty flee when no one is chasing them, but the honest and innocent are brave as a lion – Proverbs.'

The lion reference particularly made me laugh.

In life, my children had always called me their tiger; they knew I was fierce and would always protect them.

We all know tigers beat lions so I saw it as a good omen.

On that first day in court, Vijay spoke of how we'd met the Sicas as neighbours at Stafford Heights in 1993. He said the relationship with the family soured when he became aware of Neelma and Max's relationship.

'I didn't like an adult man with my daughter,' he said.

Vijay spoke of his dismay when Max asked for permission to marry Neelma.

The court heard a recording of the November 2002 confrontation between Max and Vijay at our Bridgeman Downs home, when Max asked for Neelma's hand in marriage.

Vijay often recorded conversations, and that was one of those situations.

'You don't know what I'm capable of, I'll bring you down,' Max had screamed.

'I can cave your fucking head in right now and get away with it. Capiche?'

During the hearing, Max smiled, waved, and blew kisses to his family and supporters seated in the public gallery.

Six months earlier, he'd been refused bail for fears he would flee the state.

His family's support sickened me. Yet, at the same time, I admired their strength. Family was everything to the Sicas, just like it was to the Singhs. They were protecting their own, even if their own was a cold-blooded murderer ... a monster.

I was required to attend court four or five days during the 95-day committal hearing. Each day, I'd carry a photo of my children, as well as Lord Shiva.

The days I was required to testify, I wasn't nervous or scared. However, I was sometimes confused—and amused—by the questions.

On one particular day, Max signalled the defence for a piece of paper and pencil.

He scrawled something across it and handed it back.

"So you were having sex with Max?" they soon questioned me.

I laughed.

'Well... he did call me Mum,' I said. 'Can you ask him, does he have sex with everybody he calls Mum?'

The court erupted in laughter.

The questioning by defence barrister Sam Di Carlo was relentless and nothing was sacred.

Vijay was even forced to deny claims he was responsible for our children's death and that he had framed Max.

The court also heard how in the weeks before her death, Neelma had been secretly living with Max in Bribie Island, while Vijay thought she was in Dubai.

While I'd known about this visit and obviously discussed it with Neelma, we'd never told Vijay. He got mad at me later for keeping it from him.

On another day, the defence wanted me to talk them through what I'd seen in our house after the murders.

They wanted me to tell them about Sidhi's blood on the wall.

I couldn't handle it.

'Please don't do this to me,' I pleaded. 'I've already gone through this. The way I saw them then, you're reminding me of that.'

The magistrate asked the defence to stop their line of questioning.

They also asked me about the first things I saw when I entered the house.

I told them about the strongly wrung mop and the bucket with dirty water in the laundry.

I described how I'd walked into the kitchen and saw leftover KFC boxes.

The police had pulled the rubbish out of the bin.

I told them about the soggy roof above my dining table and the chandelier falling down.

We spoke about the wooden spoon, which was found beside the spa upstairs. It had the letters VS written on it and was almost a metre long.

I often initialled our belongings, as they would get misplaced at other people's places.

For prayer sessions, I'd cook for 200–300 people in a large pot.

And the spoon, which I'd purchased years earlier in Fiji, was kept inside Sidhi's old baby cot, inside the garage.

The defence tried to say that only a person who knew where the spoon was would pick it up.

'No,' I argued. 'The spoon was very visible when you walked into the garage.'

So much was raised during the committal hearing. Religion, our finances, Vijay's affairs, domestic violence, our sexual history, my massage company.

More than 90 witnesses were cross-examined by the defence.

It was really hard. However, after you see your children like I did, not much bothers you. I was pretty numb.

I couldn't care less what was raised in court. I knew who I was, and I knew I was a good person.

Some of the stuff in the media was wrong too but even that didn't faze me. I'd just laugh it off.

My faith told me Max wouldn't get away with the murders.

We just had to go through the motions.

* * *

After losing multiple appeals for bail,[26] on October 13, 2010, Magistrate Brian Hine found there was sufficient evidence for Max, 40, to stand trial.

I was sitting at home watching the news when I heard.

'Ha, serves you right!' I squealed, dancing around the room.

I was elated, as was Vijay.

In August 2011 Max lost his bid for a judge-only trial.

'We had six separate pre-trial hearings under s590AA of the Criminal Code (Qld) which took nine months to hear. The pre-trial hearings were related to the footprint evidence, the use of experts to determine the footprint evidence, the confessional evidence against Andrea Bowman, two applications in relation to the forensic procedure orders which saw Max put on socks, place his feet in bleach and walk up the stairs, and the length of time and admissibility of the 18-hour interview with Max. We won all six pre-trial hearings, which enabled us to then take that evidence to trial. We had to hire a truck to put the brief of evidence in, it was so enormous. We went through two to three photocopiers and spent months reproducing material for the defence team. Under disclosure, we had to do this."

  —*Andrew Massingham*

CHAPTER 31

COMMITTED TO STAND TRIAL

On January 31, 2012, Max entered the Supreme Court of Brisbane, dressed in a dark suit, shirt, and tie.

Before Justice John Byrne, Senior Judge Administrator of the Supreme Court of Queensland, he pleaded Not Guilty to three counts of murder.

Prosecutors took more than an hour to read the list of more than 700 potential witnesses.

A pool of 600 potential jurors was also called.

In total, 15 jurors were sworn in that day and the case was adjourned until the following month.

The jurors—eight men and four women—held our future in their hands.

If they didn't put Max away for life, Vijay or I would kill him ourselves. That, I was sure of.

Max made an application to the state to exclude audio and video interview recordings from April 22 and 25, 2003, in the days after the children were found dead, as well as the recording from March 31, 2004, that lasted 18 hours.

Both applications were dismissed.

On February 13, 2012, the trial resumed.

I prayed to Lord Shiva, like I did every morning, and readied myself for court.

It is very hard to remember exactly what else I did that morning. It was a moment I'd waited so many years for. I wasn't scared or nervous, I knew Max would be going to jail. This was just a formality.

For the next 79 days, the Supreme Court would hear evidence in the trial of Massimo 'Max' Sica.

In a 2.5-hour opening address to the jury, the prosecution spoke of Max's manipulation and alleged:

'The children were found in a spa bath in an ensuite attached to the main bedroom. All had sustained blunt force trauma head injuries which were consistent with their having been struck with a garden fork that was found in the garage. DNA from all three was on the tines of the fork.

Stains in Neelma's bedroom matched her blood. There were drag marks in her blood from her bedroom in the direction of the main bedroom. Clumps of her hair were near the drag marks. There were other indications of a struggle.

Sidhi was killed by a blow to her head with the garden fork. Stains and spray patterns in her blood were on and around the bed in the main bedroom where at times she slept. She appears to have been killed while asleep in the main bedroom and then put into the spa.

Kunal suffered severe head injuries and was rendered unconscious when struck with the fork while asleep in his bed. There were bloodstains, spray patterns, and drag marks in Kunal's blood in his bedroom, and drag marks in his blood from there towards the main bedroom. He looks to have been taken from his bed to the spa bath. There he drowned.

The applicant and Neelma had been involved from 2002 in what the prosecution characterises as a "complicated and tumultuous" relationship. By February 2003, the relationship had broken down. The applicant had not taken well to the termination and had sought to reinvigorate it by a variety of strategies.

In the days before the killings, the applicant visited the Bridgeman Downs house more than once.

Sica then returned late on the night of 20 April 2003, or in the early hours of the next morning. They argued and he strangled her. To ensure that Sidhi and Kunal could not implicate him in Neelma's murder, he killed them too.

There had been attempts to make it appear that there had been a burglary, particularly in Neelma's room. And the killer cleaned up.'

On February 21, 2012 – day eight of the trial – we were forced to bear all of our family's secrets. The affairs, threesomes, excessive drinking, and bad business deals.

In cross-examination barrister Sam Di Carlo even suggested Vijay wanted a threesome with me and Max.

It was rubbish.

Mr Di Carlo then asked about the prostitutes, whether I masturbated massage clients, and if Vijay once had sex with his nephew's wife and taped it.

The next day, Vijay was forced to testify that he had once hit Neelma so hard with a pool cue over her leg that it broke. It was devastating but very true. Vijay had caught Neelma on the phone to Amit and beat her with the cue. She was left with black and blue bruises on the top of her right leg.

Afterwards I'd cried with Neelma on her bed.

I'd cried for our life, which once seemed idyllic, but was now a shambles.

I'd cried for Vijay, who felt it was OK to raise a hand to a woman; to beat our beautiful daughter until she was black and blue.

I cried for Sidhi and Kunal, who had witnessed the attack.

And I cried for myself. I felt helpless.

Neelma's injuries were so bad, she couldn't walk.

When I returned to school with Neelma a few days later, we explained what had happened to the principal.

I needed help and I didn't know who to turn to.

The school called police and Vijay was charged with assault.

Vijay later asked Neelma to write a letter to police saying it was all her fault. He said if he was charged, he wouldn't be able to go to Fiji to run the business… we didn't want that. In protection of her father, she obliged and the charges were dropped.

He was also questioned about hitting me.

'She was so drunk she couldn't stand…I didn't want her to damage any property,' he'd said.

CHAPTER 32

CROSS-EXAMINATION

For days Vijay was cross-examined by the defence team. It was exhausting. While prepared, Vijay and I were embarrassed and ashamed by the information being released.

On February 27, Vijay admitted to the court that I blamed him for the deaths. This was true. We'd only travelled to Fiji for the wedding of his employee. If I hadn't gone, I could have saved them, I'd said.

To be honest, I think I was looking for someone to blame. Anyone.

Under cross-examination, Vijay spoke of Max's 'goody-goody' ways.

'(He) was manipulating, brainwashing my children,' he said. 'He brainwashed my daughter ... told her to go to the school counsellor,' he said of the time Max convinced Sidhi that Vijay had molested her.

On February 28, Neelma's robbery during her time at the Pacific International Hotel was raised.

It was during this time Max wormed his way into Neelma's life. He was conniving, manipulative, a swindler. He saw dollar signs in his eyes and convinced Neelma to sue her workplace.

On March 9, Amit fronted court to speak about his relationship with Neelma.

He spoke of their bond and a meeting with Max in Brisbane's Post Office Square where Max said he had a brain tumour and would die within a month.

From the moment Max said he had the tumour in early 2003, I knew it was a lie.

As predicted, it later emerged he'd never been sick. Max made the story up to encourage Neelma to resume their relationship.

He admitted this to police during his interview on March 31, 2004.[27]

He also admitted to sending the emails about Neelma and Archana in the same interview.

Max also told Amit he was gay and that his relationship with Neelma was a ploy to convince his conservative parents otherwise.

Of course, none of this was true.

Max always had an ulterior motive to his lies.

Four days later, it was his knowledge of the unrelated plan to kidnap the Asian businessman and hold him for ransom that was under discussion in court. Max's former parole officer, Steve Arnold, told the court of Max's knowledge of a discussion between fellow parolees to kidnap the man. Max told the parole officer Neelma knew about the plan, and he was concerned about the ramifications of that.[28]

Of course, he was more involved in that situation than what he told the officer.

Again, he was always one step ahead.

For the next four months, every small detail of our family interactions, our relationships and business dealings, was discussed.

I went through a range of emotions in this time. Love, despair, loss, and embarrassment.

CHAPTER 33

THE POLICE INFORMER

Prior to the start of the committal hearing, Max filed an application under s590AA of the Criminal Code 1899 (Qld) to exclude the evidence of Andrea Bowman,[29] a lady he'd met in 1988 when she was employed at his dad's pizza restaurant.

The two of them became friends but lost contact in 1994.

After seeing Max on television talking about the murders, Andrea put a card in his letterbox. They started to meet up and the murders became a regular topic of conversation.

In June 2003 she told police she was conversing with Max and over the next two years, she relayed their conversations to detectives.

However, in October 2015, the police became concerned for her safety and asked her to stop telling them about her meetings.

Max wanted to dismiss a conversation they had on March 16, 2008, the eve of his 38th birthday.

Andrea spoke about how she'd arranged to see Max at 8 pm on March 16, 2008, but cancelled.

Disappointed they would not be catching up, he started drinking.

She later decided to see him, and when she picked him up, she said he seemed loose and unguarded.

They spent four hours together.[30]

The following is an excerpt of statements made by Andrea Bowman in R v Sica [2012] QSC 5[31]

'I suggested softly, "I know you would have wanted to kill yourself," Andrea said. "You probably thought you would – but then survival instinct kicked in. You would have hated them for making you do this. It's their fault because you would never have done it if they hadn't made you," I continued, "I just need to know you feel remorse." Max volunteered, "If I could take back what happened, I would. I have remorse for what I did." I asked cautiously, "What did you do?" Max said, "For what I did." He paused and said, "Do you know how hard it is to kill someone when someone says, 'Please don't, don't please'?" His eyes drooped heavily. He mumbled then looked at me, astonished, and covered his lips and said, "Was I just talking then?" I said no. He rested his head back on the seat again.'

Andrea didn't report the conversation to the police until 13 days later, and when she phoned them to say what happened, police said she was affected by alcohol.

In spite of this, the police obviously saw Max's comments about remorse as important and, for the first time in a long time, asked Andrea to meet with Max again and record the conversation. She agreed.

On April 22, 2008, Andrea and Max spoke in her car.

When she asked how he was feeling, he said, 'I don't feel anything anymore. That's why I drink.'

He also told her he believed a machete was used. He spoke of our house and 'blood everywhere'.

I remember feeling sick when I heard the tape.

It was like a confession, but under a veil of 'what if?' A bit like O.J. Simpson's book, *If I Did It*.

When asked in the Supreme Court if she believed Max was guilty, Andrea said she was like a yo-yo. 'I went up and down.' [32]

She said Max was 'such a nice person' at times but then a darkness would come over him. She also didn't believe Max had come to our house with the intention of killing someone, but that something went wrong and that he lost control.

'I need to do the right thing...no one has the right to get the shits and kill three people. It is wrong,' she told the court.

'Max has put his family through this [and] the Singh family have been through hell.'

Andrew Massingham on the evidence of Andrea Bowman:

'I 100% believed everything claimed by Andrea Bowman over the course of the committal hearing and trial. Andrea had worked with the family previously and was a trusted person in their family and in the Italian community. The psyche of Max Sica is he wanted you to believe he did this. He got off on talking about how the murder may have been staged, how they did so well to clean it up; that fuelled his fire. It's typical psychopath behaviour. This got him off mentally; people theorising how clever he was. It's an odd relationship to have a married woman, with children, attending parks at midnight, Max's house alone, talking about the murder of three kids. However, this went on for years. Eventually, things started to turn pleasurably towards the case, where some of his comments were sustainable in evidence.

Andrea first started contacting Max following the murders and was talking to him for three or four years before she approached police. We used a number of covert techniques to capture this conversation with her. However, Max was constantly paranoid about this and would often make her remove her clothes, glasses and footwear when they spoke. On other occasions he would 'pat her down' for listening devices. These were the games he liked to play. It was like he suspected Andrea was talking to us and wanted to thwart any attempt for us to intercept the conversation. In the end though it was to be one of his many downfalls.

Andrea was just a piece of the puzzle though, so we never put all of our weight on a confession from him. I took my hat off to this woman. She had motor neurone disease and went through ten days of committal hearing for four to five hours a day where she was absolutely exhausted. The defence tried to break her down but she'd keep fronting up. She was amazing.

Her motivation? We still don't know. Maybe she enjoyed talking about this stuff as much as Max. Maybe there was a fascination there. Normally informants are in trouble or want money. She asked for none of that. She just wanted to help.'

CHAPTER 34

FOOTPRINTS

Like the fingerprint, the footprint has its own characteristics across 26 bones, 19 muscles, and 107 ligaments, with ridges, toes, soles, and arch all offering their own unique individuality.[33]

Following the discovery of nine consecutive footprint impressions on our floor and staircase in 2003, police had built a database of some 10,000 footprints during the investigation.

On May 14, 2012, forensic podiatrist Dr Sara Jones told the Supreme Court about the footprints[34] found in our house. Dr Jones had a solid history in the industry including a diploma in applied podiatry, a master of science, and a PhD.

She had worked as a podiatrist since 1986 and had extensive experience in forensic podiatry, including analysis of footprints and characteristics of foot impressions.[35] She'd worked on more than 50 cases.

Dr Jones told the Court she'd been shown photographs of the footprints. She said the first impression at the base of the steps was sufficient to get measurements of length and width. Other impressions were only partial of the toe and ball of the foot, or too faint to get any measurements.

The court saw a comparison chart between a left foot impression and Max's left foot; his measurements were similar on several. A partial impression taken of a right foot at the scene was also consistent with his right foot on two variants.

She told the court while she was unable to exclude Max as a match, she said this did not mean he was (or wasn't) the person who had killed our beautiful Nim, Kunal, and Sidhi.

Max's lawyers questioned whether the replica of our staircase, which detectives had built at Petrie Police Station, was an accurate reproduction.

Detective Sergeant Zitny told the court the staircase was reproduced by the same people that built our house.

They'd also used the same type of carpet, although it was not from the same batch.

Robert Kennedy,[36] a Canadian crime scene specialist and former Canadian Mountie and authority on morphology, also fronted the Supreme Court a couple of weeks later.

Mr Kennedy had experience in identifying people through their footwear.

He was well known for his work on a number of big cases overseas including that of Allan Legere, a Canadian rapist, arsonist, and serial killer who'd murdered at least five people, and who was known as the Monster of the Miramichi.

Dr Kennedy told the court he'd also examined the prints and compared them to ones obtained from Max during the investigation.

'I found there was support to the hypothesis that the impressions could have been made by this foot,' he said.

Andrew Massingham on the footprints:

'There were nine footprints in the house the police were interested in; one full footprint and eight partial. These were socked foot impressions in bleach, applied to carpet. Max was clever enough to wear socks, as do most criminals that commit break and enters, they wear them on their hands. The footprints were found by the fingerprint guys when they placed newspaper on the carpet to stop the fingerprint dust from falling. When they picked up the newspaper, they saw a full impression of a foot on the carpet. The forensic investigators then returned to the scene to look at the stairs. The full impression was at the base of the stairs. Then, there were prints on every second step – where he'd taken two at a time, his foot flat and hanging off the step.

We went to the local universities to gauge the thoughts of podiatrists, who pointed us to a senior university lecturer in podiatry at the University of South Australia, Dr Sara Jones, who referred us to Robert Kennedy, a retired former sergeant of police in the Royal Canadian Mounted Police. Kennedy had devoted his life to examining things that had come into contact with each other. He had a database he had self-built of 40,000-50,000 footprints. His methodology was that no two footprints are the same and he did a lot of work around shoes, or footwear that were left at the scene of a crime, that he would then match to a foot by looking at pressure points and the size of the foot, for example.

Initially there was a lot of scepticism about the relevance of this science; people were pretty doubtful as to whether it was even a process, let alone if it was something we could use to convict someone of murder. There had been praise and criticism of it, in both the states and Canada. We had so many questions for him. How can you? It's on carpet? It has fingerprint dust on it. What about the underlay on the carpet? If someone was carrying a body up the stairs, what would that do to your foot—would it squeeze it out … and make it appear bigger? There was a lot of doubt around the science. However, when we spoke to this guy on the phone, he came across as brilliant; he was such a professional. We decided to bring him out, maybe six months after the murders.

We had to re-build the staircase with the company that had constructed the Singh's home. They had to re-build the stairs for us, with the same carpet and underlay. We then had Max wear thin, medium, and thick socks, stick them in a bucket of bleach, and force him to walk up some stairs. We had to apply for a court order to do that, and we were successful. Max was cooperative but did try to undermine the science throughout. Kennedy examined the foot impressions and concluded there was a high degree of correlation between the foot impression and Max's foot. We then did a graphic overlay of the foot impression and Max's foot and they were damning. The defence objected to their inclusion in court. However, the judge said we could give the jury an impression of the footprint on the carpet, with an acetate of Max's actual footprint—the jury could then put one over the other and draw their own conclusion.

We also took foot impressions from Vijay, Shirley, and Archana, along with all other persons we could place as visiting the house prior to the deaths. In addition, we constructed a database of 10,000 odd footprints to prove the unique nature of foot impressions for the use of Kennedy. We acquired these from volunteers who visited the police exhibit at the annual Brisbane show, the Ekka. We showed Max his foot impressions during the interview on March 31, 2004. During that record of interview, we questioned him about the footprints. His comment was, "You can't prove it's mine." Wouldn't your response be, "Why do you keep questioning me about this?" We found this fairly interesting.'

CHAPTER 35

THE IMPACT

As the trial neared a close, Vijay, Archana, and I were asked to complete our Victim Impact Statements. In these statements, we were told to speak from the heart, explain the impact of what Max had done to us and how his callous and torturous crimes had forever changed our lives.

It wasn't easy putting pen to paper about the devastation he had caused us, the nightmares, arguments, and confusion, and the family and business losses endured. However, I always loved speaking about our children and the joy they brought us in life.

The following Victim Impact Statements were read to the Supreme Court, prior to sentencing on July 5, 2012. A doctor's report was included with my statement, as was a summary of hospital discharges. Ten pages of sketches Kunal had made were also submitted to the court.

Victim Impact Statement – Shirley Singh

I, Shirley Singh, mother of Kunal, Neelma, and Sidhi Singh, have no words to explain the effect of the violent crime that has been done to us.

I lost my flesh and blood, my three innocent children without any reason, or say, an accepted reason.

If it was because of drowning, a house fire, a road accident, drug overdose, there would have been a reason. But what happened to them was no reason at all. They never hurt anyone, harmed anyone, or annoyed anyone, except me, sometimes.

They were happy, loving, caring, and full of humour. How can anyone so cold-blooded do what was done to my children? Nim and Kunal had seen the world a bit, but my baby Sidhi was defenceless.

While sleeping with her blood on the wall and the floor, did she try to get up to defend herself? That vision is crystal clear in my eyes today and will always be there. What I saw of my children and how I saw, I pray to God, no mother will see what I saw.

I will never forget the telephone call I received in Fiji on the 22nd of April 2003 at 7 pm Fiji time, the caller telling me that my children had been shot.

The caller made three attempts, I was very rude and didn't believe them. After making numerous calls to Brisbane, I was asked by Archana to get home as soon as possible.

I tried to ask her, but all she said was to come home. I was horrified. How I got to Brisbane, I don't remember. After the flight, I remember asking everybody, even the man at immigration, if he had seen the news and if it was true about the Singh children being shot.

I remember buying DKNY perfume, which my son Kunal had asked for.

Kunal and Nim's laughter still rings in my ears as they said goodbye to me at Brisbane Airport. I dropped my hand luggage on the escalator and they were standing there laughing and drawing attention. They would look or find any excuse for laughter and I loved acting dumb just to make them laugh.

The children that I last saw laughing, I was taken to identify. I could recognise my son, but I couldn't recognise Nim.

I asked them why is she so black and why is her stomach big?

I was then told she was in the spa with hot water running over her. As for my baby Sid, I couldn't recognise her.

As I am writing this, my heart breaks. I could still see them that way. I was traumatised.

How cruel and inhumane, inhuman, cold-blooded monster, evil spirit, maggot, could do such a thing?

We are the Lord's creation and no one has the right to destroy it.

My belief is no matter how hard one tries, they can't escape two types of justice. Criminal justice and universal justice, that one cannot escape.

I, as a mother with faith, believe that.

I then had to go through my house, which was so difficult and also impossible. I froze, I could barely talk.

My son's room, which was his heaven, I saw my son's blood on his bed.

My heart is pounding rapidly as I am writing this. He called me his tiger.

But his tiger wasn't there to protect him.

Then Nim's room, which was her pride.

My daughter always stood up for me and I wasn't there for her.

My—our—room had a king-size bed, which would fit me and my children so we could sleep together and watch TV together.

It now had bloodstains behind the wall and on the bed head and also on the floor.

My Sid slept there that night and her blood was everywhere.

My baby always slept with me. That night I wasn't there. The sadistic coward wouldn't dare do that if I was there.

My ensuite, I used to have fun, drink wine, listen to music with Nim and Sid, was turned into the graveyard of my children.

Even after suffering through heartbreaks, I held my marriage together so I could provide the best for my children.

On the 13th of May, the day before the funeral, I went to spend some time with them. I was told not to go and see them closely; it might haunt me. How could I not go? I am their mother. They are my children.

I am crying while I am writing this, I so much wanted to touch them, but was scared as I did not want to hurt them as their skin was burnt.

I can see now what I saw then. Every tear that I dropped and am still dropping will be listened to, one day.

It is very difficult and hard to explain, what and how I felt on the 14th of May, the day of the funeral.

I didn't know what I was doing or saying, I was telling everyone my children were coming home.

I was up all night and kept looking at the clock, even after taking two Stilnox. I started telling my friends and relatives there for support, to 'get up and get dressed and start tidying up, my children are coming home, but no one is allowed to see them.'

I didn't want anyone to see them the way that I saw them. I always kept my children clean, groomed, and well dressed and always smelling beautiful.

My children did come home. But in coffin boxes. My three children, Kunal, Nim, Sid, came home in coffin boxes.

Can anyone understand or feel what I felt as a mother when I saw them in the coffins?

I still sit in the formal lounge most afternoons, facing the door, imaging Kunal driving up the driveway, with Nim and Sid giggling or laughing over something.

The Lord is very powerful. He can make it happen. He sends them in my dreams. Why not in reality?

They say hope and faith is the thing with feathers which perches on your soul and prays with silent tears that never stops.

On the 14th of May, my children were cremated. I tried to stop everyone but no one would listen. I lost it. I was forced to sit down and wait for my children to be cremated. Can anyone imagine what it is like as a mother to sit and wait? People tried to comfort me, but I pushed them all away. I didn't want anyone to even touch me.

After this as we were going home, I looked up and saw the smoke. The smoke of my children being cremated. I was distraught. Vijay came home and I was so angry at him, thinking how could he let them cremate our children. If I had my way, I would have embalmed them and kept them with me always.

I went upstairs and found Sid's pillow. I held it and cried my heart out. I then wrapped it in plastic and held it in my arms. I asked her for forgiveness for not being there and sang her favourite lullaby song and slept with it.

I did this every night until the pillow was taken away from me.

My relatives consoled me and told me I had to be strong, because we have to do our 13 days of mourning and prayers for peace for our children. How was I to do this? How could I be strong? After the 13 days, we had to move so our house could be renovated. While staying in a motel, we saw a story on 'A Current Affair'.

Max was saying on national television how he found my children and described the causes of death.

I was so frustrated, angry, paranoid, I lost it. I started drinking heavily, two bottles of red wine, to make myself numb. It never worked, so I took Stilnox as well.

When I came back home, after the renovations, I felt so much pain in the pit of my stomach, I felt loneliness, the emptiness, I yelled and screamed and called out for them to come home.

I then made up my mind I would not live in this emptiness and started putting up their pictures everywhere so that I could see them. I did their rooms, dressing them with their photos on their beds, so I could see them in there.

I set up the spa, which I took as my children's grave. I light a candle every night in the spa, so they are not in the dark. Especially for Sid, who always slept with the lights on.

I set a shrine downstairs and I light a candle which has been burning, exactly like me, for nine years and will never stop.

That's my life.

I started feeling their presence, I still do. I am living with the thought, the belief they are still with me. I cook for them, change, wash and iron their clothes.

I still celebrate their birthdays, except this year, the important birthday, Sid's 21st. I haven't done anything, but I will, soon.

After this horrific incident, I was so shattered, I didn't know what to do or how to deal with my life. I stopped applying makeup, I didn't have my hair done for more than three years, I haven't been to any parties or weddings for the past nine years, I have isolated myself from the Indian community, because they were asking me many questions about what they saw or heard in the media.

I gave up their favourite foods, KFC, chicken burgers, Sizzler, which was Sid's favourite. I only went back to Sizzler once, to take her friends for her 13th birthday.

The supermarket was a horror for me for more than three years because I couldn't stand to see the aisles with Breaka, Coke, chips or biscuits. I still have Kunal's last can of Coke, half finished. I kiss it every now and then. I still have Sid's Breaka, which I bought before going to Fiji. I stopped eating meat after how I saw them.

I no longer go to funerals as I cannot stand to see coffins, except on one occasion.

Drunk and after taking some Stilnox, I would walk to the cemetery, at 2 or 3 am, searching for them. I once passed out in the local park, Sid's favourite place, when I was looking for her.

On the 4th of August 2003, Kunal's 19th birthday, I was emotional; then someone calls and tells me that his wife is pregnant and having a boy, who will replace Kunal.

'What? No one can replace my son!'

I was so angry, I took Stilnox, I filled the spa with water and went in. I tried to kill myself in the place where my children were put.

December 29, 2003, Neelma's 25th birthday, I celebrated and crashed a few days later, ending up in a mental health hospital. Sid's 13th birthday, 4 March,

2004, I was so frustrated, without rest, once again, I tried to kill myself.

I wanted to burn the house down and myself too. Once again ending up in a mental health hospital.

The delay in justice was explained and I was asked, would my children be happy in the matter I was acting?

From that day, so I don't hurt my children, I promised myself I won't be silly and I will be strong for my children.

Until today, I have been standing strong in my house, with my children and happy memories.

Even though people have asked me how I am living here, my answer is 'how can I turn my back on my children after what has happened to them?' What will they think of me and their tiger? I am not a coward.

My family was closely bonded. Archana, 'Sonia' my eldest daughter, was the mother figure and in control.

Nim, Kunal, and Sid had so much respect for her, they would rather listen to her than me and I loved it.

My daughter Sonia was shattered, left alone without her brother and sisters. She is married, the mother of two boys, and lives in the same world as me. She thinks they are still home. She buys them presents, wears Nim's clothes, and walks around the house.

God knows how she feels deep inside. I ask myself why they are not here, too.

Life would be so different. My house would be full of joy and lots of grandchildren. I still wonder what I have done to deserve this punishment of loss. All say it is a life imprisonment of grief and loss for myself and Sonia. It was so heartbreaking watching her with her first child. In our custom, the whole family and relatives welcome a baby with laughter, dance, and celebration. But my daughter Sonia and her husband sat there all alone with me and my Vijay. I managed to help her control her emotions for a couple of days. A few days later, she was very emotional and once again felt the impact of missing her brother and sisters at such an important time in her life.

Neelma was dignified and courageous, ambitious and with self-esteem. She was always caring and loving. She studied business management, so she could assist her father and get a good job so I wouldn't have to work. Nim always stood by me, always protected me when things weren't good. She hugged and held me and told me that things would work out for my good one day.

To cheer me up, she would tell me I'm the best mother in the world, and she would only leave her children with me to babysit, no one else.

I miss the times she would open a bottle of wine, put on some music, and dance funny to cheer me up. She was a sister and a friend, as well as a daughter. My heart aches as I write this.

Nim mothered Kunal and Sid. She always paid extra attention to Sidhi. Sidhi was like a living doll to her. Neelma was 12 when Sidhi was born. When Neelma was home, I had nothing to worry about with Sid, because she would bathe her, feed her, and carry her around. After feeding her, Nim would wipe her lips and neck, apply lotion and talcum powder so she would smell nice, just as I always did to all of my children. Sometimes, I would ask her to study and to let Sid sleep. Nim did this even though Sid was 12 years old. Grooming, kissing, and hugging her.

Neelma made me buy our dog Bujo, a mini fox terrier. She said he would always look after me and be good company when she was not there. Even now Bujo goes into Nim's room and cries every now and then. I wish he could talk.

As for Kunal, he was a very special boy, born in a very special way.

He was born exactly nine months after we had an eight-day prayer session for Lord Shiva at our home in Fiji.

I didn't expect to get pregnant, but after having Kunal, everyone regarded him as a gift from the Lord Shiva to me. Always gentle, kind, and caring and he would listen to me every time.

He would rub his chin on my cheeks and say you are the best mum in the whole wide world. I'll always look after you and marry someone like you.

My loss is tormenting and it is hard to explain. Kunal, an ambitious, creative person, he made sketches of the front fence, he wanted to include a water feature in the front yard and went to buy a water feature statue which is still standing out the front of the house.

Kunal had plans for a spa on the patio to cover up the backyard, so he could enjoy the sunup. He drew sketches of cars and wanted to be a designer. When I reminded him that his father has a business, he decided to do business management first, so he could help his father with the technology.

I have been deprived of all my dreams my son had for me. He had a huge sense of humour, always making everyone laugh and a big cheeky grin and a good bloke. So, his friends used to call him 'Chicko'. The echo of his laughter still rings in my ears and I always tell people about the joyful life we have.

The impact also extended to Kunal's girlfriend Katrina. She was left heartbroken.

She would come and visit me with bunches of flowers, lock herself in his room, and cry for hours.

Sidhi Singh, 12-years-old, my baby, came forcibly into my life. I was on the contraceptive pill when I conceived Sidhi. Losing her is like someone stabbing and pulling my heart out and leaving me lifeless. I felt that pain for all of them. But as for Sidhi, I can't explain, she was my baby.

When she was born, I said to Vijay, I will have company after Sonia, 14 years old and Neelma, 12 years old at the time, are married. She always clung to me, asked for hugs and slept with me. I remember saying to her, can you leave me away for a while, especially when I was busy, and I regret saying that, because now she has left me alone for good.

She was always active and playing. She loved her friends and doing things for them. I remember one morning at 5 am, I woke to find her in the kitchen, making a loaf of sandwiches to take for her friends, because they were going on an excursion that day. Sid also took 18 packets of chips and drinks for everyone.

I never got angry when my children did this. I quietly smiled to myself and felt proud. I am thankful for all her friends'—children of the age of only 10, 11, or 12 then—support up until today. After the incident, it was so heartbreaking to see them come every now and then and spend a day in Sidhi's room.

Even today they are still very supportive to our family. When I hug them, I feel as if I am hugging my Sid. Sidhi was always happy, joking, and making fun of my mistakes.

She wanted to be a singer. She said, 'Mum, once I release a disc, you won't have to work and you will be treated like a queen with servants.' I remember she used to make her listen to her sing a song from the movie 'Titanic'. *'Near or far, wherever you are, you'll always be in my heart and my life will go on and on.'* So true.

I am going on and on and on, still carrying the coffin boxes on my shoulders for justice. After the tragic loss of my children, my life has been turned upside down. I lost interest in everything. I am living because I have to live. I had to work because I wanted to remain in the house until I get justice. At the committal hearing, I was accused of many improper acts. It was very hard to defend myself when everybody in the community asked me if this was true. What can I say? I would tell them that they should consider my loss instead of thinking of the stories they heard in the media. I felt that I was the accused and not the victim.

At present I am not working, since December, because I could not work because of the trial and I would not be able to concentrate. The trial has been extremely difficult. I was prepared to disclose all of my personal details, including our dirty laundry, to the police, but I never imagined that we would be scrutinised to the extent that we were, that our personal life would be made public and that we would be asked the same questions continuously. Not realising that I was there for the justice of my children, and not to talk about sex scandals. I felt a discrimination of my Lord Shiva and my culture.

Whatever I've stated in the victim impact statement is the truth and nothing but the truth, I swear on the name of the Lord Shiva.

For my most loved children, Neelma, Kunal, and Sidhi Singh.

May the road rise to meet you, may the wind be always on your back, may the sunshine fall on your faces, may God hold you in the hollows of his hands, until we meet again.

—**Shirley Singh**

Victim Impact Statement - Vijay Singh

To your Honourable Judge

On the evening of April 22, 2003, our lives were torn apart when I answered the phone and found out something terrible had happened to our children.

Right now, as I write this statement, those awful feelings and memories are coming back even stronger.

Losing a loved one is a great pain to bear, let alone losing three, it is a greater pain, too big to comprehend.

How could he take their lives the way that he did, to take the young and vulnerable, those who could not protect themselves? He did not have any feeling or love for another human being.

It feels like a dream, as well as a nightmare.

It doesn't feel real, doesn't sound real, but every day that we don't see them, we know that it is real.

There is not a single day that goes by without us talking about them. We shed tears every day; it has become a routine of our lives.

Because of this man's actions we've each been given a lifetime sentence of loss and sadness. What wrong or harm did my children do to the accused, who so callously and cowardly ended their lives?

They deserved the right to live their lives to the full. We had the right to watch our very young Sidhi grow up into an adult, mature, and realise her potential.

Our Sidhi was so sweet and lovely, good at making friends and being very active as well. She was our baby.

I can still remember the pain we went through in 1995, when a piece of concrete brick fell on her foot and she was at the Royal Brisbane Hospital. She was just barely five years old. Myself and her mother Shirley did not sleep the whole of that night, and stayed right at her bedside.

It was so difficult to bear the pain, though so small an incident.

How can we bear the pain of losing her and her brother Kunal and sister Neelma, forever, never to see them again?

Kunal was a well-behaved and respectful son of ours. He was a sociable boy, with so many friends.

He promised he would follow my path into the automotive field and assist with my business. He was very knowledgeable on the technical side of the automotive industry.

Neelma, a very caring, loving and above all, very ambitious and smart daughter that no one can replace.

She was also very protective towards the family. She always appreciated my efforts in providing everyone's needs as a father, being also concerned about my financial commitments as well.

Losing our children has shattered our lives forever. We will not see them ever again, for as long as we live. Our hearts suffer from the deepest wounds that will never heal.

Since 2003, I have developed some medical conditions, become a diabetic and heart patient.

In October 2003 I was diagnosed with a heart problem and subsequently a stent was placed (in the heart).

As a result of this procedure, I am now on several medications for life, since then, for my condition.

Prior to this family incident I had been a very active sportsman, playing senior level soccer and golf from the age of 15.

The tragedy has destroyed us financially as well. I could not concentrate and conduct my business in Fiji effectively since the incident, and as such had to sell my assets, etc., at a loss in 2005.

Our investment properties were put on sale by auction here and dispersed as repayments of the borrowed sum that were difficult to meet.

We live in the house that was built for my family and presently are finding it very difficult to manage that.

I've been working here in Australia since 2006, but not earning enough to meet our requirements.

My wife Shirley could not work for a year after the tragedy and thereafter only on an on-and-off basis for seven years. She hasn't worked since December 2011 owing to this trial and presently finding it very difficult to go back to work because of the emotional stress.

The effects of the tragedy have taken its toll on our relationship as well. We tend to argue and blame each other for the loss of our children.

For the last nine years we have ended up in magistrates court a number of times to settle our matters. We remain to live in the same house, with the fondest memory of our beloved children.

Our faith and beliefs have kept us going as we pray every day to get justice for our children.

The person who murdered our children is a maniac, a sadistic killer, not acceptable in this society.

Respectfully prepared by Vijay Singh, father of the children.

Victim Impact Statement – Archana 'Sonia' Pathik

To the presiding judge,

My life has never been the same since the 22nd of April, 2003. When a request was placed to write this document, I felt nervous and very ill, sick in the stomach that nine years of suppressed emotions have now surfaced, which I have been dreading ever since.

Nine years, the worst news was presented to me, that horrible phone call on the 22nd of April, 2003, a call that gave me an asthma attack while I was trying to make sense of it all, during that moment. Now my life has and will never be the same knowing my two beautiful sisters, Neelma and Sidhi, and my one and only brother, Kunal, are no longer with me.

When I was asked about how old, and how tall and their date of births, I knew something was not right and then it all became a reality when I was told three bodies had been found that were similar to the physical description I had been given.

I was in a great deal of shock, I was then requested to identify the bodies, which I chose not to do, despite being the only next of kin present at the time. Ma and papa were away on a business trip overseas,

How can a 26-year-old go through what I did? My parents were angry at me for not being there, for protecting them like I was supposed to. I initially felt like I was a suspect and made a disconnect from my own self and I started blaming myself. I hated myself and felt I was unworthy of any love and affection, I'm the eldest and I was the protector.

To walk through the house, after it was released to me and my papa, Vijay Singh, I will never forget the sight which has become a constant nightmare which I have had to live with for the rest of my life.

The blood splatters of my baby sister, my angelic Sidhi, on the walls of the room, made me feel really sick, even writing about it. Mentally scarred, it is a sight I will never forget.

The blood of my siblings had been shed, our own blood had been shed, how can someone like me ever forget this?

The trauma I face still to this day and walking back into that room and walking into the bathroom to light the candles in the spa, makes me still, to the present day, sit there and just look, gaze at the loss involved.

I was requested to assist with the funeral arrangements, which I had no idea how I managed to get through. I was breaking apart but I knew my parents' wellbeing was a priority for me.

Saying goodbye to three coffin boxes, sitting right in front of me, I was having no idea how to react, was something I constantly think about. I know what it feels like to be numb, lifeless, and confused, no feelings, no emotions. I wanted to cry but no tears will fall. I want to be angry but my mind and body were not permitting me to be that way.

Neelma and I had planned always to be there for each other.

I felt and still feel that I failed her. I let her down, I let my Kunal and Sidhi down. I still haven't forgiven myself and slowly burn inside from time to time when I let go. I become very ill. Things would have been different if they would have been here, today with us.

My minds races back and always thinks this, that if I would have been there then this would have not happened.

But seeing the state of the house when released and after reading the post-mortem report, if I was present then, I would not have been writing this right now.

My security became an issue for my husband and it was decided we should leave Brisbane and move somewhere that could give us some security and some peace of mind.

I thought of the city where my sister Neelma and I were planning to live in. The dreams that we had, what we would achieve in this city.

After she had grown successful in her role that she was trying to gain, she wanted to relocate, so she could leave her past behind her and move on forward.

Once the move was decided upon and finalised, I was looked upon as someone who was a coward. My own parents disowned me and called me by those names.

My papa stopped speaking to me, my community also said I was a coward, selfish, and this really hurt me on top of everything else I was mentally and emotionally going through.

My relationship with my parents became very estranged. They chose not to speak to me. My wellbeing was not their priority and I, at this stage, was not a priority. I became a forgotten child.

This was taken away from me and I hated to accept that. I was the eldest and only child left. I am still saddened by this right now, because this is not the way things were meant to be. I didn't know how to grieve.

My relationship with my husband became strained. Two very loving beings and best friends, living the life of strangers under the same roof. Both living separate lives, but together, trying to make sense of it all. How do we grieve? How do we support each other? How do we support my parents?

I became pregnant and felt very happy, left with another loss and then two more failed pregnancies after that.

I started to give up. My heart was just not letting go, I hadn't given myself time to heal. I didn't accept the fact that my sisters and brother would never come back. Once I accepted this, I could breathe properly. I could cry, I could scream from the top of my voice and say 'why me, why us, why this pain, why this situation?'

I questioned my faith, I fought with my gods and questioned them. I lost my faith, I stopped believing, until my fifth pregnancy gave me hope, after I was 20 weeks pregnant.

When I held my son after he was born, all I could hear were the voices of Neelma and Sidhi, telling me they would be there in the delivery room supporting me through this. My eyes searched for them, my ears wanted to hear them, I was so angry in this joyous occasion, that they were not there, they were not with me. I felt so alone and I felt so lost. My firstborn and I were doing this all alone. I held him and cried and thanked God for blessing me with him and asked God to give me the strength I need right now, give me the courage to see this through and give me the blessings to be a good mum.

On special occasions, celebrations, birthdays or Hindu festivals, I miss them dearly. I cry from time to time, but always celebrate their birthdays every year, cutting a cake and placing sweet offerings on their shrine at home.

My kids know and acknowledge them all the time. They also light candles and place incense on the shrine. We always talk about how it would have been if we all would have been together.

Neelma and Kunal, their partners and kids and Sidhi growing up to be a young, beautiful woman.

When we look back at childhood photos of Sidhi and Kunal, my kids are shocked to realise how similar they looked in features and this has happened a lot with cousins and even my parents noticed.

This was traumatising for me in the early stages because I knew what Kunal and Sidhi looked like when they were babies and growing up, as my mother did.

It was a blessing, but at the same time it hurt very much.

I still to this day question how someone could be so cruel. What runs through a person's mind to act with such cruelty, especially to my beautiful baby sister Sidhi.

She was only 12, she was my beautiful, sweet, and innocent baby sister, who I held in my arms from the day she was born and from that day forward and I looked after her so well.

She would always pick up the phone of her own free will and tell me everything. She would sleep over most weekends and she was the one who suffered the most pain and was taken away from me.

I question this all the time. Her blood splatters on the wall still haunt me, why was this so?

Does this person have any remorse? Does this person have any feeling? This person is a cold-blooded murderer, a cruel and sadistic cold-blooded animal who has caused enough grief, pain, and suffering for as long as I live.

My life will never be the same, nor will I ever forget the ongoing pain and suffering I had to and still have to live with forever.

The physical link has been broken and is unmendable. They will not come back to me. Life will never be the same, as I dreamt it to be, or wish it to be.

Mentally and emotionally, I have to take it a day at a time and for the last nine years, be the support, rock, and armour for my parents which has challenged me in so many ways.

I have also seen my mum through her suicidal phase, where a few attempts were made which resulted in hospitalisation and police coming to the hospital.

The most severe case was when she took a few Stilnox tablets, filled the spa where my sisters and brothers were found and drank a bottle of red wine and sat in the spa to drown herself. This happened right in front of me. The police were called, an ambulance was called, and this is another scene I can't release from my mind.

I am a mother now. I felt her pain right from the day I gave birth. This is not fair on anyone who was close to my siblings.

This has been taken away from us.

Respectfully,
Archana Pathik, Sonia, elder sister of Neelma, Kunal, and Sidhi Singh.

CHAPTER 36

THE JUDGEMENT

'When the victim impact statements were read, there wasn't a dry eye in the court. I was hoping he would get 45 years. Either way, I was so relieved he was guilty. Will he ever get out? I hope not. He's a parasite, a manipulator, and an asshole that has to answer for what he did. In this lifetime, and the next. Without equivocation, he should be there for the rest of his life.'

—**Bryan Paton**

'I think the jury took their time to go through the evidence. They took their role very seriously. They had a lot to consider. There was no room to sit in the court on that final day. It was the biggest relief I've had in my life. Had it have gone the other way, I don't know how I'd have coped, how Shirley and Vijay would have coped, or how she would have gone on. To have seen him acquitted, we wouldn't have been able to cope with that.'

—**Andrew Massingham**

On July 3, 2012, the jury entered its fourth day of deliberations. I had a good feeling the jurors would make the right decision but the decision was in their hands.

Every morning and night I would pray to Lord Shiva for justice. I would ask him to destroy the evil, that had destroyed my life. I would also pray to the Goddess of Strength, Durga, to help me stand strong.

I was positive Max was going to be found guilty.

On July 5, 2012, Justice Byrne delivered his judgement.

Nine of the jury returned to hear Justice Byrne deliver Max's sentence.

The Crown detailed Max's previous crimes, which until then, had been relatively untold.

In 1993 he had been jailed for nine years for setting fire to the Ashgrove Police Station and Shailer Park High School, and for the attempted arson of the Red Hill Police Station. He was jailed again in 1997, while on parole.

Of course, we knew a lot of this, but the public and jury didn't; many seemed shocked.

I was disgusted this type of person existed on this earth, and more so that we had once associated with him.

I sat in the second row, behind Max, as the judge readied himself.

Max stood with his hands behind his back. He looked defiant and unforgiving.

SUPREME COURT OF QUEENSLAND

Citation: R v Sica (2012) QSC 184
Parties R v Sica, Massimo
File No/s: BS68/11
Division: Trial
Proceeding: Sentence
Originating Court: Brisbane
Delivered on: 5 July 2012
Judge: Byrne SJA
Order: As per sentencing remarks
CATCHWORDS: CRIMINAL LAW - SENTENCE - SENTENCING
ORDERS - CUSTODIAL SENTENCE - LIFE SENTENCE
- GENERALLY - where accused convicted of three counts
of murder - where accused on parole when committed the
murders -where a non-parole period of 35 years was imposed
for the three counts of murder
COUNSEL: B Campbell for the DPP
S Di Carlo for the defendant
SOLICITORS: Director of Public Prosecutions for the applicant
Legal Aid Queensland for the respondent

[1] Massimo Sica,

[2] In the middle of the night of Easter Sunday 2003, you went to the home of the Singh family.

[3] Neelma Singh was expecting you.

[4] Her brother, Kunal, aged 18, and sister, Sidhi, just 12 years old, were also in the house, probably asleep.

[5] Something happened in Neelma's bedroom between the two of you.

[6] Enraged by jealously most likely, you strangled Neelma with both hands, using sustained pressure for about a minute, intending to kill her.

[7] To ensure that Kunal and Sidhi would not tell that you had murdered Neelma, you murdered them too.

[8] You struck their heads with the tines of a garden fork, inflicting multiple blows with severe force.

[9] Neelma was probably dead when you struck, and disfigured, her face with the garden fork.

[10] You put your victims into the spa bath in the master bedroom ensuite.

[11] Your savage attack on Kunal had rendered him unconscious. He drowned after you filled the bath with water and covered the three bodies with bedding.

[12] These are brutal, horrific crimes—in the worst categories of murder.

[13] You set about covering your tracks.

[14] You cleaned up to some extent, using bleach.

[15] You implemented other measures to deceive the police.

[16] The deception you practised included using your own children, taking them to the house on the Tuesday afternoon, when you pretended to discover the bodies.

[17] You are manipulative and deceitful; and the pretences continued.

[18] A couple of examples may be mentioned.

[19] You feigned distress in making 000 calls and later that Tuesday during an interview with the police.

[20] Much the same thing happened when, during a walk-through of the house on Anzac Day, you presented yourself as overwhelmed by grief.

[21] And you lied—often: in particular, when you asserted that you were at your own home that Easter Sunday night.

[22] You were 33 years old at the time, on parole, with a criminal history that includes serious offences.

[23] You have no remorse whatsoever. Your only anxiety is for self-preservation.

[24] Illustrative of the absence of any remorse is this; since the killings, by your deliberate conduct, you have consciously added to the agony of the Singh family; as examples, you had it insinuated that Mr Singh may have instigated the killings, which is despicable; and, at the committal and at trial, your defence raised publicly matters of private concern with, obviously, a significant potential to humiliate Mr and Mrs Singh and Mrs Pathik; matters that, as you well knew, had nothing to do with the murders. Such misconduct tends against leniency.

[25] The murders have had devastating consequences for the Singh family.

[26] The victim impact statements of Mr and Mrs Singh and the surviving sibling, Mrs Pathik, reveal the awful miseries that they have experienced in the last nine years, and point to the suffering that they will endure for the rest of their lives.

[27] I have had regard to the factors specified in s.9 of the Penalties and Sentences Act 1992, including those listed in sub-section (4), in deciding on the minimum non-parole period.

[28] I have also taken into account totality considerations, which require the Court to examine the overall behaviour involved in the three murders in deciding on a just, appropriate non-parole period. Totality considerations operate as an ameliorating factor.

[29] Still, your offending is so very grave that it must be met with condign punishment.

[30] Massimo Sica,

[31] You are sentenced: for the murder of Neelma Singh, to imprisonment for life; for the murder of Kunal Singh, to imprisonment for life; for the murder of Sidhi Singh, to imprisonment for life.

[32] Pursuant to s.159A(3) of the Penalties and Sentences Act 1992, I declare the 1,299 days spent in pre-sentence custody from 29 October 2008 until 13 November 2008, and from 30 December 2008 until today to be imprisonment already served under each of those sentences.

[33] Pursuant to s.305(2) of the Criminal Code, it is ordered that you must not be released from imprisonment until you have served a minimum of 35 years imprisonment, unless released sooner under exceptional circumstances parole under the Corrective Services Act 2006.

CHAPTER 37

JUSTICE

Max's sentence of life imprisonment, with a non-parole period of 35 years, was the longest term ever handed down in Queensland.

The prosecution used the sentence imposed on South Australian triple murderer Jason Downie as an example.

He'd been given a non-parole period of 35 years after killing 16-year-old Chantelle Rowe and her parents in a brutal knife attack in South Australia in 2010.

After Max was sentenced, the judge asked if he had anything to say.

'Well, I didn't kill no one and the Queensland justice system is corrupt, OK? Sorry, that's all I have to say.'[37]

I watched as those around the court shook their heads.

I was so angered by his response. He had no shame, no remorse, and no regrets.

All I wanted to do was hurt him. I wanted to pull his hair, shake his head, and spit on his face.

The only thing that I got out was an attempted spit. I lurched back and launched it forward, as far as I could.

It was like the movie 'Titanic', where Jack taught Rose how to spit. It was pathetic. It went up in the air and landed flat, only centimetres from where I stood.

'If you don't know how to spit, don't spit,' my friend Angie squealed at me, laughing.

I apologised profusely to the lady in front of me. 'I'm so sorry, I didn't mean to.'

Next, I tried to jump the seats.

I wanted to punch him, just once.

I swear security didn't even flinch; they just watched me.

Next, I grabbed the detectives who had worked so hard on the case.

'I don't know whether to thank you, or to worship you,' I said, cuddling them.

Tears rolled down my cheeks. I was overcome with emotions.

Grief, relief, gratitude.

I was happy it was over.

As security led Max from court, I stood and watched. I wanted to make sure he was gone.

Soon after, Defence Lawyer Sam Di Carlo approached me.

'Mrs Singh, you're a very dignified person … I'm really sorry I had to do that.'

'You were just doing your job,' I responded.

Carlo also tried to approach me—his arms outstretched like he wanted a hug. Security swooped in very quickly, removing him from the court.

Outside, he told reporters his son was innocent.

'If I believed that my son had been capable of that … I would say to the judge, "give one hundred years,"' he told reporters.

He then read from a prepared statement.

'I have spoken to Max, and while I'm stunned by the decision, we maintain he's absolutely innocent,' he said. 'We will continue to defend those charges at appeal …'

Earlier in the week, Anna Maria had screamed at the waiting media.

'How am I going to cope? You will see how I'm going to cope. Do you see me cry? You not see me cry. I am like my son and he is innocent! I know my son! I know my son! The police in this country covered evidence!'

That night, we were joined by family, friends, and media at our house.

I couldn't stop crying. I was happy it was over, but I still couldn't wrap my head around why it had happened in the first place.

It was the end of a very long chapter.

* * *

We had lived and breathed this investigation, while grieving the deaths of our children for nine years. We had our darkest secrets put under bright lights and rolled out via tabloid.

While I was first embarrassed, I learned to live with my truth.

After all, it was *my* story.

Justice had been served and that was the ultimate goal.

In August 2012, Max's brother Claudio offered a $270,000 reward for information that would clear Max's name.

'Max was in bed,' he told Australian Associated Press on August 2, of the time the murders took place. 'I believe that the police just chose to believe what they wanted to believe.'

Claudio also claimed crucial evidence, including fingerprints, was never mentioned in the trial because of the costs of investigating them.

'Innocent until proven guilty is just a nice phrase in the legal textbook,' he said.[38]

Max's wife Shiv also said she'd never questioned Max's innocence and would continue to fight to clear his name ... or wait for him to be released.

'I will be maybe 70,' she said.

On September 2, 2013, the Queensland Court of Appeal rejected Max's claim that his sentence was excessive.[39]

'The wilful killing of a child is regarded by society with particular abhorrence,' the court found. 'Neelma, Kunal, and Sidhi Singh were deprived of the possibility of having long and fulfilling lives. Their parents and surviving siblings were deprived of their companionship, love, and support. Instead, as the sentencing judge found, they were condemned to lifelong misery and suffering.'

On April 11, 2019, Max lodged a petition with Governor of Queensland Paul de Jersey for a pardon, or referral of his convictions to the Court of Appeal under Section 672A of the Criminal Code (Qld). The matters were refused in December 2020.

He later applied for a Statutory Order of Review, claiming the governor may have been 'predisposed' against him. He also said Attorney-General Shannon Fentiman showed apprehended bias when she decided not to refer his petition to the Court of Appeal.[40]

The latest was dismissed in November 2021.[41]

CHAPTER 38

THE HARD YARDS

The Queensland Police Force gave this case their all over nine very long years.

From the moment I was wheeled off that plane, to the moment the verdict was read, they relentlessly pursued justice for my children.

I am eternally grateful for the time they gave us, our children, and the case. I know how hard it was on so many of them. The impact on their lives and those of their families, particularly in those early days.

The things they saw at my house will never leave their memory.

The conversations they had with me, Vijay, Archana, forever imprinted in their minds.

Officers like Bryan Paton were even sidelined during the case.

'In November 2004 I was told I was too close to the investigation, too involved. To me, I was totally committed to the case. I was providing the support I believed necessary to the Singh family. How could I not be close to these people, how could I not be emotionally involved? This was my life for 20 months. I had a Christmas card from Shirley in December 2003 that said "You're my only hope for justice." That meant something to me. The District Officer told me I was to have no further contact with the Singhs unless I had a senior officer present. In December 2004, I was told to take two months leave. I went home quite distressed. I felt like I'd let everyone down. I was later diagnosed by a psychologist as clinically depressed. I also lost my eyesight during an operation. I never went back to the force.'
—Bryan Paton

In total, the police had pursued 1,500 lines of inquiry, 750 witness statements, 490 exhibits, the elimination of 180 DNA profiles, and the collection of 10,000 foot impressions across five-and-a-half years.

In 2013, Detective Senior Sergeant Zitny and Detective Inspector Massingham were awarded an Operational Commissioner's Certificate from Queensland Police Commissioner Ian Stewart for their 'considerable efforts' to solve the murders.[42]

'The case will undoubtedly etch an unforgettable chapter in the history of crime in Queensland as one of the most cowardly acts of violence ever committed upon innocent children,' Detective Inspector Massingham told *The Courier-Mail* at the time.

'We are honoured to have been part of a very dedicated team of investigators and forensic experts, both sworn and unsworn, that worked tirelessly to see justice for a family that had suffered an incomprehensible loss. The graphic nature of the crime—we have three innocent children that were murdered in their own home—that sort of investigation stirs people to bring about a successful conclusion.'[43]

Andrew Massingham on the personal impact of the case:

'The Queensland Police Service wanted to get it right but what came with that was the human cost. Nine years later, there was a skeleton of staff standing in the court when that guilty verdict was handed down. I started on the case as a junior and finished the case as one of the senior members—and that was just because of the toll it took on people.

Why did I stick it through? I couldn't walk away from it. I wanted to see justice for the family but it was more than that to me. It was a challenge for me personally; I didn't want to see this case go unsolved ... whether that took five months or 20 years, I wanted to get it done.

As I saw more and more people leave the job or go to other challenges, I became even more certain I wanted to stay and to support Joe. I didn't want to walk away from my mate. What we went through together on that job, we'll never see again.

We had a largely circumstantial case where people were always going to question "is it enough?"'

The size and scope of the case was overwhelming and there were definitely days we thought it may never be solved.

The level of scrutiny of evidence from senior executives (of the Queensland Police Force) was massive.

If we had have gone too early, say, in the first or second year, instead of waiting until five or six years, would we have got the same result? I wouldn't be as confident.

The DNA issues were big players, we also didn't have the Sica confession to Andrea Bowman. There were key things that came about, due to the longevity of the trial; things that made it stronger. This ate away at some of the officers on the case, who wanted to walk him down the aisle in that first or second year. It caused angst. But in the end, we got the right result, for everyone.'

CHAPTER 39

CATCHING A MURDERER

To ensure a conviction, police exhausted every possible lead in Max's case.

They were in touch with the US Secret Service, Canadian police authorities, Fijian communities, former and current clients, partners and associates of each and every possible suspect.

Of course, none of this was known to us at the time.

Below are Andrew Massingham's insights on some of the key actions taken during the investigation.

On the investigation in Fiji...

It was unbelievable what we had to do in Fiji, and Arveen Singh—who was the liaison officer for the case—was pivotal to this. During the committal hearings, a theory arose the murders were a 'hit' from Fiji, based on Vijay's previous affairs and business dealings. We had DNA profiles in the house we couldn't match to people, and had to investigate. These people were pig farmers with two pieces of iron over their head; they lived in shanty towns. Joe and I couldn't just walk into these communities. These were the husbands or boyfriends of women that had had affairs with Vijay, who potentially may have had a motive to kill Vijay's family. This is what (Max's barrister) Sam Di Carlo was throwing up after the committal hearings. Arveen would drink kava with these people, in order to access the community. These are people that didn't know what DNA was ... and we were asking them to give a specimen of saliva. Arveen was pivotal in this part of our investigation. He'd previously worked with the Fijian police before coming to Queensland.

On the use of international agencies, like the US Secret Service...

Neelma had an old Nokia phone that we took to the US Secret Service twice. They were able to further examine the phone, which was beneficial as we were able to enhance the text messages sent on the night of the murders as well as a 'phone call she had recorded on the handset between her and Max regarding him having a brain tumour. The US Secret Service had the best technology, with labs based in Hawaii and Tulsa. They were cutting edge with everything they did and were instrumental in assisting us with access to that phone.

On the discovery of Max on RSVP...

When we had Max under surveillance, we identified that he had four separate RSVP profiles. He'd then often have multiple women on the go at once, that he was sexually involved with. Most of them were young and he'd generally target girls that had no support networks. We would follow him to each of their houses. We had to interview each of them and get a statement from them and it was tragic when his true identity became known to them. At one stage, I even placed a profile online. I was a detached single female who had been in an unsuccessful relationship and was looking for a new guy. I pretended I was educated at the University of Queensland with a science degree. Within hours Max hit the profile. He sent a picture of himself on a bed, with no shirt on. We were aware that previously Max had sent this same picture to at least one other female and attached to this picture appeared to be some form of spyware that gave him a level of access to her computer. We were aware this was possibly a strategy he used so we had to ensure our covert methodologies weren't compromised. I even completed an assignment, which I left on the desktop of the computer I was using for him to find in case he was able to remotely access the computer we were using. That profile enabled us to introduce an undercover detective to Max, who formed a relationship with him to coax a confession—which never happened. This never went to trial as it wasn't part of our evidence.

On Max trying to alter the children's time of death...

The fact the children were found on the Tuesday, meant the assumption was made by the media they were killed on the Monday. This was crucial, as Max's family provided an alibi for him for the Monday. When we could determine they were actually killed on the Sunday, his family then went about trying to construct an alibi for him for the Sunday. He tried to say his brother and parents were home and that he didn't leave the house but it didn't fit. Neighbours reported hearing shots on the Monday night, the day before the bodies were found. One witness said they heard a volley of shots, another said they heard single shots. When the first police arrived at the scene, Max said he had three people in a bathtub. He told police it looked like they'd been shot. Next thing you know, the ballistics team was at the scene. When the bodies were x-rayed, there were no bullets. When we searched Max's Honda, in the centre console was a starter's pistol. This was the mindset of a guy who was trying to cover his tracks, of how he was thinking. We don't know why the pistol was in the car, he must have forgotten it was there. So why was all of this important, you ask? He was trying to alter our calculations on the time of death, to give himself a watertight alibi. The water in the bath was at 37 or 38 degrees when the body was found. Either the water had been running the whole time, or it had been turned off, then more hot water had been dumped on them when Max 'found' the bodies. His former wife, Sara Davidson, said Max was fascinated by 'CSI'. She said he watched and recorded every show and went on a website that told you how to remove fingerprints, how to remove DNA, what police do at a crime scene. She said to us: 'There's a particular episode he really liked, death in a spa bath or something.' The closest we could find was a 'CSI' episode called 'Altar Boys' about a young woman who dies in a sauna. It looked at how heat could affect the calculation of time of death. This didn't make it to the jury, but it was something we had to follow through. The hot water was also a tactic of the killer.

On Max discovering the bodies...

Max said he entered the house through an unlocked rear garage door, which police allege was at 1:56 pm on April 22, 2003. His son Daniel later told police he believed his dad had unlocked the door, possibly with a key. Max said he searched downstairs before following the family dog, Bujo, upstairs. However, painters say they saw him pass the dog out to his two children in the backyard. Despite saying he'd planned to meet Neelma and the children to go to the movies, Max could never tell police when the arrangements were made … and we could never link that to any communication. Max made a phone call to 000 at 2:33 pm on the afternoon he found the bodies. He told them, 'I've got three dead bodies in a bathtub.' Police initially located two bodies. The third, we said, was hidden by bed linen and foam on the top of the water. The police searched the house looking for a third body. When Neelma was found, she was only wearing a T-shirt, nothing else. Kunal and Sidhi were wearing night attire, consistent with what they would wear to bed. There was evidence in Kunal and Sidhi's room they were attacked in bed, and we said, while they were asleep. Taking into account the use of Neelma and Sidhi's phones, the house alarm, and the last communication with Neelma's phone at 11:10 pm, we placed the time of death as within a few hours of 11:10 pm. Max attempted to call Neelma's phone maybe once or twice following their deaths. This was a very different pattern of communication than between him and Neelma in the lead up to their deaths. On Monday April 21, 2003, Max made an effort to give himself a rock-solid alibi. He rang up mates he'd not spoken to in ages and asked if he could catch up. He went to shopping centres where he could be captured on CCTV. He very much went about writing a strong script for himself on that Monday. He then tried to coax us into believing the murders occurred that day, and the media ran with that.

On the crime scene…

Police found no forced entry to the Singh property. The point of entry that night (the rear garage door) was the point of entry regularly used by Max to enter the house. There were no defensive wounds on any of the bodies; no sign of a struggle. It all happened very quickly. No disturbance or noise was recorded by any of the neighbours. There was also the act of manual strangulation, which was common with domestic homicide incidents. During a break and enter where there is a clear intent to do serious harm to a person the offenders usually bring a weapon to the house; this did not occur in Max's case. This was a disorganised crime and one which was not pre-planned. There was also the knowledge of the house security, the dog, alarm and sensor lights (which had been turned into the 'off' position). If Max was coming over, Neelma would turn this light off. We said that meant he was expected.

Max also had a knowledge of the house layout, that the victims would be in bed asleep, upstairs, and that Sidhi usually slept in the main bedroom. We say the killer spent a fair bit of time in the house on the night. They mopped and staged a crime scene. To us this meant the killer/s knew something very important—and that was, that they weren't going to be disturbed. If this was a random act, they would kill and then leave the scene as quick as they could because they didn't know when someone was going to come home. But this killer knew that no one was coming home. There was also the communication between Max and Neelma that night, and the expectation of a visit. Kunal wanted friends over, Neelma had told him no, she wanted a quiet night— we say that is because she knew that Max would be coming around. Masala tea was also on the kitchen bench. That tea was only used by Neelma when Max came to the house. Also, the prayer documents found in the house and the use of the garden fork, which was hidden amongst other garden tools in the garage. Blood of all three victims was found on this fork. One of the tines was bent, and two of the outside tines appeared to be cleaned. The murder weapon was not brought to the scene but there was a knowledge of where it was kept. The investigative team believed the fork was a ceremonial choice as Lord Shiva often held a three-tined fork. As such we placed some significance on that choice of weapon. The mop was put back in the garage, leaning up against Sidhi's cot—this was out of position to where it was usually put (lying across the barbecue out of reach of the dog). The bucket of bleach was on the laundry floor. The bleach bottle was under the laundry sink and had Neelma's blood on it. The bed linens from Neelma's bed were in the spa. Her body had been dragged, from her room, on the doona, to the spa. Bleach had been poured over her head because Max often spoke about his belief that police could lift fingerprints off human skin. Neelma's bedroom drawers were pulled out over the blood on the floor. The killer had tried to make it look like a burglary, like someone had ransacked the place. This wasn't a situation where someone had been interrupted in the act of committing a murder. This was staged after the crimes were committed. Cash, laptop computers and other valuables were left untouched. Open jewellery boxes and jewellery were found on top of bloodstains on the floor. The killer deliberately did this. Kunal's remote control was also placed on his own blood trail as well. Kunal loved his TV. Neelma loved her jewellery.

On the use of CyberScrub...

We raided Max's house pretty soon after the discovery of the bodies. At 9:35 pm on April 22, 2003, police opened the computer at the Sica family home in Trouts Road and found a program called 'CyberScrub' running. This was a fairly advanced program that essentially erased everything on your hard drive then ate itself. It had previously been used by the US Armed Forces. However, Max had an old version of Windows on his computer and as a result, his computer was taking a long time to do what it needed to do. When Queensland Police seized the computer, we were able to identify that the program was on there, that it had been downloaded on a certain date and that it had been engaged. He started the program working at 8:03 pm on the Monday night (April 21, 2003), so after the children's deaths but before the bodies were found ... a fairly significant find.

On Max's behaviour/lies...

Max told a multitude of lies during the investigation. These related to his relationship with Neelma Singh, the distribution of the lewd emails, the brain tumour illness, the CyberScrub program and the time spent at the crime scene on the day of discovery. To us, the motive of his behaviour or lies was a realisation of guilt. People that constantly lie in relation to key points generally do it for a greater purpose. Max's behaviour was never consistent with him being a secondary victim. He was always very confident; there was a bravado about him. During the committal hearing, the defence team tried to paint him as a victim, they said police had stood over him, interviewed him for 17 hours, that we were trying to break him down. That was the flavour they tried to create. He was good at crocodile tears too. This was particularly relevant during his walk-through of the crime scene on April 25, 2003. When he got to Neelma's door, he got the shakes. The tears started and he claimed he couldn't go on. His dad escorted him from the property where media was waiting to take his photo. It was all a sham, an act. He even punched a glass window in the main bathroom out of anger.

The safe story...

Following the murders, we found a safe, located in the main bedroom, with the door left ajar. This was Vijay and Shirley's safe and while this was not a significant find at the time, the safe came into play many years later. As part of our DNA testing on the property, we had tested a carpet square from the garage. This square sat underneath garden tools, including the fork which was used during the murders. It had also previously sat underneath the barbecue. With advances in technology, this square was re-tested many years later. The square came back with two unknown male profiles, so we had to start the process of identifying who that DNA belonged to. We found that one of the profiles belonged to one of Kunal's friends, who had come to a party at their house. However, we did not know who the other unknown profile belonged to. In late 2006 or early 2007, we received an email from the police DNA results unit to say there had been a hit between the unknown male profile number two and an exhibit that had just been brought into the government chemical laboratory. They said there had been a safe dumped at the back of a suburban shopping centre in Toombul, on the north side of Brisbane. Alongside the safe had been some bloodstained tissues. An assumption was made the safe was stolen and the burglar had injured themselves during the robbery. When these bloodied tissues were tested, there had been a DNA hit between them, and the unknown male profile two on the carpet square. It was a mind-blowing result that required significant follow-up. We decided to go back through Shirley's massage client list and run a ruler over all massage clients. We did a full analysis of the clients and took some more DNA profiles. On December 20, 2008, we got a hit. It was a 75-year-old bloke who had been a massage client of Shirley's. He'd had a hip operation and the orthopaedic surgeon told him that in order to get his hip back in order he needed to start riding his bike. So, he took his bike down to the velodrome behind the shopping centre for a ride. A snake came out of the bush, he fell off his bike, and he injured both knees. He walked to the toilet block where he used toilet paper to wipe his bloodied knees. He then threw the paper in a nearby bin. Ibis birds then picked that bloodied tissue up and transferred it 50m to where the safe was then dumped the next morning. The safe was not connected to the blood. It was crazy. We had essentially closed the last unresolved chapter.

Just over a week later, at 5:24 am on December 30, Max was arrested for the murders of Neelma, Kunal, and Sidhi.

CHAPTER 40

A QUESTION OF PAROLE

I have thought of Max often since he was sentenced.

I'd love to say I haven't, but I have.

While he may be in prison, he still gets to live his life.

He gets to talk to his family, his children.

He gets to breathe, to dream. He may not have parole until 2047 but honestly, how quickly do the years go?

In 2047 Neelma would have been 69, Kunal 63, and Sidhi 56.

Archana would be 71.

They'd have got to experience so many things in this time. First loves, first cars, birthdays, Christmas, holidays, engagements, marriage and babies.

It may be many years until he's out, but Max still gets to do all of that. My children don't.

In December 2021 Max's son Daniel was jailed for five and a half years for drug trafficking. Apparently, he was caught with 11.753 grams of pure methylamphetamine when a search warrant was executed at his unit.[44] They also found cocaine.

In court, Justice Paul Freeburn said Daniel had more than 400 phone messages from 29 customers relating to the supply of the drug.

Police also discovered a $50 counterfeit note and more than $35,000 in cash.

His barrister said he was dependent on drugs at the time and was 'associating with the wrong people.' They also said Daniel was seeking 'geographical isolation' to get away from the crowd.

Of course, he was immediately made eligible for parole.

I found this really sad. Only five years prior Daniel had been charged with contravention of a probation order, fraud, and traffic offences, including unlicenced and drug driving, failing to stop, and driving without due care and attention.

He'd also been mauled by a police dog after attempting to run from police during a traffic intercept.[45]

I had to think ... isn't this where Max started? With the 'pettier' crimes – drugs, arson, robbery?

And yet, here we are, continuing to suffer, day in, day out.

Our lives are forever changed by the actions of this man.

In 2016, the Queensland Parole System Review[46] was undertaken by Walter Sofronoff QC.

The review was ordered following the murder of 81-year-old Elizabeth 'Beth' Kippin by Anthony James O'Keefe in Townsville.

O'Keefe had killed Beth in an ice-fuelled rampage which saw him charged with one count of murder, two counts of attempted murder, one count of burglary, one count of wilful damage, and one count of threatening violence. He had been released on parole only 12 hours earlier.

The review sought input from victims' organisations, organisations working with offenders, academic researchers and experts, interested members of the public, and persons working in the criminal justice system.

As a result of the review, Queensland Premier Annastacia Palaszczuk announced major reforms to probation and parole services across the state.

The government accepted all but two of the review's 91 recommendations with more money committed to Corrective Services staff, as well as rehabilitation, drug, alcohol, and mental health services.

I was never asked for my opinion on probation or parole in Queensland, but I wish I was.

I'd have told them that people on parole should not be allowed to stay at home or roam around in the night. At the very least, just like the community is advised of the location of child sex offenders, we should have been given the courtesy of knowing Max's criminal history, particularly as he was on home arrest.

Had we fully known about his crimes, we would not have gone near him.

Psychiatry analysis had shown Max was capable of 'psychopathic' tendencies. To me, this meant he was capable of hurting people.

Just like Adrian Bayley, who murdered 29-year-old Irish woman Jill Meagher in Brunswick, Victoria in 2012,[47] or Rosie Batty's ex-partner Greg Anderson, who beat and stabbed their son Luke to death at a Victorian cricket club in 2014,[48] Max had a long criminal history.

If I had it my way, people like Max would be hung from a tree, above a fire while chilli cooked on a pan.

He would endure intense pain and suffering.

He shouldn't get the comfort of prison. He should have been locked in solitary confinement, or on a farm, forced to work for a living.

Instead, he's in a prison where he gets to enjoy food, exercise, and earn money.

To me, that is unfair.

In February 2016, it was reported Max had struck up a friendship[49] with Gerard Baden-Clay, a man convicted for the 2012 murder of his wife, Allison. Max and Gerard had been spotted walking around the yard together at Wolston Correctional Centre, on the outskirts of Brisbane.

Daniel Morcombe's killer, Brett Peter Cowan, is also there.[50]

Max has been described as a 'model prisoner' by those in the know, something that bothers me a lot. Good 'model citizens' don't murder people. Good 'model citizens' don't set fire to police stations.

Good people have respect for the law and don't say 'the justice system is corrupt.'

Over the past 20 years, I've had a lot of time to think about what we could have done differently, how I could have protected my children better.

But the truth is, I did everything I could to love and nurture them.

I did everything I could to protect them.

I'm forever grateful to the police officers, ambulance officers, doctors, nurses, media, and Australian public who supported us throughout the years—and ultimately whose lives this affected—thank you for your love and support.

To the people that walked up to me on the street to ask me how I was. To the strangers that left flowers and cards on our doorstop. To the lady that helped me complete my groceries when I couldn't face walking down the aisles to buy products I once bought for my children. You didn't take money from me and even bought me a bunch of flowers. You were so kind.

To our extended family and friends, who were there with us every step of the way, and to my best friend, Angie Power, for her friendship, love, and laughs through the years—you helped keep me sane. You were an angel sent to me from God. I'm forever grateful you were brought into my life.

If it wasn't for my faith and the kindness of these people, I wouldn't be here today.

I honestly thought life had thrown everything it could at me, but my strength was about to be tested again.

I would soon farewell my beautiful Archana.

CHAPTER 41

TOGETHER AGAIN
February 1, 2020, 7:30pm
Melbourne, Victoria

When Kavin called from Melbourne on a Saturday evening in February 2020, I greeted him in my usual happy way.

'Hello, mister! What are you doing, how are my grandbabies?'

Silence. He was crying.

'It's Archana,' he said. 'She's in the hospital. She fell down and she's not in a good way.'

He relayed the same to Vijay.

'It's serious. She has damage to her brain; you need to come here immediately.'

We landed in Melbourne only hours later. We travelled to the Alfred Hospital, where we were led to Archana's room; she was in ICU.

When I saw her, I froze. She was on life support, so still, so silent.

I pushed myself onto her bed and lay beside her.

My beautiful Archana.

Earlier that day she'd been working at the Melbourne Convention Centre when she had collapsed in a critical condition.[51] Doctors were running tests and would provide us with news soon, they said.

Her hospital room was filled with people that night. A colourful assortment of men and women from all around the world—Filipino, Vietnamese, Indian, Chinese, Thai.

There was chanting, singing, prayers, and healing beads. Some of her friends massaged her legs and arms, willing oxygen back to her brain, while others read the Bible or shared memories of better times.

We even sang a rendition of 'Dancing Queen' by ABBA at 1 am; it was our favourite party song.

We told her we were going clubbing. It bought back memories of the parties we'd had through the years.

At Archana and Kavin's wedding in Fiji we filled the Civic Auditorium beside Suva Harbour with 750 guests. The tables were overflowing with flowers, the pillars wrapped in tinsel.

And their wedding reception in Brisbane with 300 of our Australian friends at The Greek Club.

One of my favourites was a celebration at our house on New Year's Eve 2002, the last night I ever partied with my children.

I had such fond memories of that night. Friends, family, drinks, food, dancing, singing, laughter. It was what we did best.

While not everyone was allowed to stay in the hospital room that night, I was not going to leave Archana's side. I wanted to be there when she woke the next morning, I knew that would make her happy.

The nurses gave me a gown, a toothbrush, a blanket, and a sandwich, and set up a bed for me.

I didn't sleep a wink.

The next day was a rotating door of visitors, prayers, songs, and stories.

Archana had still not woken.

Doctors asked if she was an organ donor. She wasn't. I was missing the signs, the reason for their questions.

They soon requested a meeting with us.

Archana had a brain aneurysm, a bleed on the brain, they said. Her life support would need to be turned off.

I remember looking at my grandsons, Sharaav and Vishesh. Only 14 and 12, they'd already gone through so much in their life. Their mother, with whom they were so close, was now departing them.

I lay beside Archana once more. I knew we had only hours.

Vishesh soon asked to do the same. 'I want to cuddle her, just like you,' he explained.

He lay there for an hour, speaking to his mum. 'Ma, why won't you wake up? Why are you not talking? When are you coming home?' It reminded me of my relationship with my dad when he passed.

Soon after, Sharaav asked to do the same.

I then cleared the room for Kavin to have his time. An hour later he was still there, his arms intertwined with hers.

At 8 pm on Monday, February 3, Archana's life support was turned off.

Vijay and I were distraught. While he and Archana had not spoken much in the years before her death, they'd always been so close growing up. He was so proud of all she'd achieved and loved her dearly.

I was glad I was given those last moments with Archana but I still felt robbed. *Why Archana? Why our family? Where did I go wrong?*

Vijay and I had now lost all four children we had together; so fast and so cruel.

Archana's funeral was held on May 7. She was 43.

Archana was smart, kind and caring, and very protective of her family and friends.

She loved cooking and entertaining, and she really liked helping people.

She was an ambassador for Mental Health Australia and volunteered for Rotary and the National Homeless Collective. She also worked with domestic violence shelters.

She was a nervous soul though, and it didn't take much to raise her anxiety. I'd say that came from what she'd experienced in life.

I really can't put into words how it felt to lose her. It hurt.

As a parent, you always expect to outlive your children. You take pride in watching your children succeed and watching them grow old.

However, we had once again been robbed of that joy.

Did I question my faith? Sure.

Did I wallow in self-pity? Definitely.

But I soon realised there was something greater at play; something that gave me a sense of peace.

Archana was with her siblings.

The four of them together, again.

CHAPTER 42

MEMORIES

I will never get over the deaths of my children.

I will forever live with their memory, proud of who they were.

Today, I still live in the house where my children were murdered.

Each night, I light a candle for them. I talk to them and lie in their bed.

To others this may seem weird, but to me this is life.

I have never felt scared in the house, even following their deaths.

To me, our house feels peaceful. My children were good spirits, and the house is one filled with happiness.

In the years that followed the children's deaths, Vijay and I split as a married couple. Putting aside the mental and emotional strain that comes with losing your children, we were no longer compatible.

In fact, we hadn't been for many years.

We did everything we did for the love of our children. The masquerade was now up. We continue to co-exist under the same roof but we are not in love.

On some days we struggle mentally, emotionally and financially. On others we thrive.

It's really not very different to how we lived as a married couple.

I have dreams of one day living by the ocean, while Vijay would like to return to Fiji.

I find being by the water peaceful. Following the deaths of the children, I would often travel up and down the Brisbane River by ferry, before sitting on its bank for hours, staring at the water.

Water means a lot to Hindus as Lakshmi, Lord Vishnu's wife, comes from the sea.

So that's my ultimate dream.

However, at the moment I don't want to leave my children.

Nor does Vijay. I think this is why we still call our Bridgeman Downs house home.

Family is more important than anything. When you bring children on to this earth, you have a responsibility to give them the best life you possibly can.

Vijay and I have fought like cats and dogs throughout our lives. However, he too lost his children and lost his business.

Because of the love I have for the four beautiful children he gave me, I'll forever love him and we will always look after each other.

As the years go by and as we grow older, I can't even fathom the thought of splitting everything and starting a new life. I have never properly worked since the incident and with Vijay unable to return to Fiji for at least six months after the deaths, our business collapsed.

Archana and Kavin moved interstate, then Archana died. Our two grandchildren, now without their mum.

Watching them grow up gives me so much joy, like the joy I had when my own children were alive.

I also regularly speak with Janel, he's a beautiful son.

He also has two children, Jaydan and Ayanah.

While they live in Sydney, we try to see each other whenever we can.

Our health is starting to fail us.

On September 29, 2017, I even had a heart attack. I had six blocked arteries and doctors placed a stent in one of them.

On November 29, 2017, I had open heart surgery.

'If everything goes well, you'll have another 35 years in you,' doctors said.

'Oh good,' I told them. 'I just need another 30 so I can welcome the dickhead that murdered my children as he leaves prison.'

Vijay also has a stent. He had a heart attack six months after the children were murdered and a second on June 27, 2022. With the latest, he had three blockages but refused surgery.

Doctors told him to eat better, slow down, and reduce stress.

'Heartbreak,' I later told him. 'That's what caused it. You need to mend your heart.'

Do I fear death? No.

With what I went through, losing four of my children, I couldn't care less if

I died today. I'd get to see them, and that would be amazing.

To be honest, once the doctors said I was OK after surgery, all I could think was, 'Bloody hell, I went halfway to heaven, and came back!'

To others that may sound morbid but to me, that's my life. I live every day with the knowledge I am one day closer to seeing my children again.

I will never know why Max did this to our family. Our family had not harmed anyone, they were lovely and friendly. He attacked the most vulnerable and defenceless.

My whole life I have stood up for myself, I've remained strong.

I've weathered the world's fiercest storm and come out the other side.

I take each day as it comes and remain committed to living a life my children can't.

Sometimes people ask me, 'How do you do it?' and I tell them: 'Memories. The past beats inside me like a second heart. I'll forever live life in their honour.'

SHIRLEY'S STORY

THE TIMELINE

DATE	EVENT
May 14, 1879	The first of Shirley's ancestors arrive in Fiji on board the Leonidas, a labour transport ship that departed Calcutta, India on March 3, 1879.
April 27, 1951	Shirley Singh is born.
July 2, 1952	Vijay Singh is born.
March 17, 1970	Max Sica is born.
October 1970	Shirley is kidnapped from an Independence Day festival in Fiji.
January 1971	Shirley and Maan marry in a traditional Hindu ceremony. They officially separate three years later.
September 21, 1971	Janel is born.
August 14, 1972	Janice is born.
December 10, 1976	Archana is born.
December 29, 1978	Neelma is born.
September 1979	Vijay starts Unique Motor Parts.
March 20, 1981	Vijay and Shirley marry.
April 27, 1981	Vijay and Shirley move to a new home in Namadi Heights in Suva.
August 4, 1984	Kunal is born.

May 14, 1987	Lieutenant Colonel Sitiveni Rabuka staged the first of two military coups to re-assert ethnic-Fijian supremacy in Fiji following the election of an Indo-Fijian dominated government the month prior.
September 25, 1987	Rabuka leads a second coup in Fiji.
1989	The Sica family move to Trouts Road, Stafford, a suburb of Brisbane.
March 4, 1991	Sidhi is born.
June 2, 1992	Rabuka is democratically elected as the country's third Prime Minister.
May 27, 1993	Max is sentenced to nine years imprisonment for 83 offences.
October 8, 1993	Max seeks to appeal the sentences imposed on him in May. The application is refused.[52]
October 31, 1993	The Singhs move to Trouts Road, Stafford, from Fiji.
October 1997	Neelma starts speaking with Amit Lala. They begin a relationship several months later.
October 15, 1997	While on parole, Max throws a Molotov cocktail at a West End unit complex. He is returned to prison for attempted arson.
October 1997	Vijay Singh assaults Neelma with a pool cue after she lied about speaking with a boy on the phone. He is charged with assault and served with a three-year good behaviour bond and fined $1000.
January 24, 1998	Archana and Kavin marry.
1998	Psychiatrist Dr Ian Curtis writes in a 1998 report that Max suffers from 'gross immaturity and high impulsivity, with antisocial features.'

January 1999	Shirley begins working from home as a beauty and massage therapist.
August 13, 1999	Neelma flies to Fiji to work as a training duty manager at The Raffle Tradewinds Hotel and Convention Centre.
December 29, 1999	Neelma turns 21.
June 2000	Shirley travels to Dunk Island to visit Neelma who has started working there.
December 2000	Neelma and Amit end their relationship after Neelma tells Amit she wants to work for an airline.
May 21, 2001	Max is released from prison on parole. He gained computer education in jail.
July 21, 2001	Neelma is robbed at knifepoint while working at Brisbane's Pacific International Hotel as a Guest Services Agent
September 9, 2001	The relationship between Neelma and Max commences.
February 21, 2002	Neelma travels to Dubai to complete training as a flight attendant for Emirates.
March 2002	Vijay denies Max's request to marry Neelma.
March 2002	Neelma has a fight with one of her roommates while at Emirates training school.
April 11, 2002	The Singhs move into their new home in Bridgeman Downs.
May 3, 2002	Neelma returns from Dubai and lives with Max at Bribie Island.
June 16, 2002	Neelma returns to her home in Bridgeman Downs.

August 9, 2002	Neelma admits to her mother she has been seeing Max. Her family strongly disapproves of the relationship and Shirley tells Max to leave the family alone.
September 2002	The family purchases a Jack Russell terrier. They name him Bujo.
October 2002	Neelma and Shirley travel to Fiji and confront one of Vijay's mistresses, Karun.
October 30, 2002	A phone call is received at the Singh's Bridgeman Downs home from an unknown person. The person tells Vijay they know where he lives and that they are going to rape his wife and daughter. This call is discovered as a message on the home message bank by police on the days following the murders.
November 23, 2002	Vijay says Max threatens to kill him and accuses him of sexually abusing Sidhi.
November 2002	Relatives of the Singh family and members of the Fijian Indian community receive an email with the subject line *"Introducing the true Sonia Pathik."* The email contains a photo of Archana on a bondage site and a sexual advertisement profile.
November 2002	Kunal graduates Year 12.
February 13, 2003	Vijay receives an email on his business computer in Fiji from a 'Peter Pan.' It was titled *'Vijay mama - baat'* and refers to a sexual liaison between Neelma and an employee of Vijay's company.

February 19, 2003	Police allege there is a relationship breakdown between Neelma and Max. From February 19 to April 13, 2003, police allege Max and Neelma only met in person around two times. 'She was very off him by this stage,' Andrew Massingham later says.
February 23, 2003	Vijay receives a second anonymous email threatening him.
March 6, 2003	Max allegedly emails photographs of Neelma, naked and handcuffed to a bedpost, to her family, including her father. They are sent from an anonymous email address with the subject, 'Neelma Singh – Introducing.' Police later say the photos were taken at a unit owned by Max's parents at Bribie Island, in February 2002. He later denies sending the photographs, claiming his computer was hacked.
March 7, 2003	Neelma starts saving all text messages in her phone. At the time of her death, Neelma had 170 messages saved in her inbox, with 144 of those being from Max.
March 15, 2003	Max alleges he has a brain tumour and needs to meet with Neelma. Neelma ends her relationship with him. In a text message he tells her: *'It's hard to tell u everything when u keep hanging up. I have some stuff I really need to speak to u about. I haven't got long left Nim, I'm sick.'*
March 27, 2003	Vijay and Neelma visit Stafford Police Station to report threatening behaviour by Max.

March 29, 2003	Neelma records a 14-minute phone conversation between herself and Max where he talks about having an inoperable brain tumour and wants to commit suicide.
March 31, 2003	Vijay installs an alarm system at their Bridgeman Downs home.
April 8, 2003	Neelma speaks to Dr Rachael Jabs from the McDowall Medical Centre, telling the doctor her ex-boyfriend has told her he has a grade four inoperable brain tumour and has only months to live. Neelma tells the doctor her ex-boyfriend has been acting strange and that he has destroyed all the letters, scans and x-rays relating to the tumour because he doesn't want his family to find out. Dr Jabs tells Neelma that she doesn't believe her ex-boyfriend is telling the truth.
April 13, 2003	Vijay and Shirley fly to Fiji for the wedding of one of Vijay's staff, Artish Sharma. The wedding will be held in Suva on April 27, 2003.
April 13-20, 2003	Phone traffic between Max and Neelma increases.
April 18, 2003	(10 am) Neelma, Kunal and Sidhi arrive at their older sister's Archana's house at Wavell Heights for breakfast.
April 19, 2003	(10 am) Shirley calls from Fiji and speaks to Neelma for what would be the last time.
April 20, 2003	(8:30 pm) Archana speaks to Neelma on MSN messenger. Neelma says 'I have to go...there is someone at the door.'

April 20, 2003	(8:56 pm) Neelma sends Max a text saying 'Will see you tonight and then chat. I think I'm coming down with something. Feeling like a day before u get sick. Will give the one ring.' Police allege the 'one ring' was code to Max that he was OK to enter the house, as the kids were asleep.
April 20, 2003	(8:56 pm) Max calls Neelma back after receiving the text message. He later alleges that during that 2 minute and 26 second phone call with Neelma, she says she is too sick for him to come around.
April 20, 2003	The 'one ring' phone call occurs. There is then a phone call from Max to Neelma for 34 seconds. This is the last recorded contact between the two.
April 21, 2003	(2 am) A resident of nearby Pepper Street is having a cigarette out the front of his house when he sees a blue or dark silver four-door sedan in Grass Tree Close. He says the vehicle has a spoiler and mags. Max had access to two cars on the night of the murder, a grey Honda Prelude and a black Nissan Bluebird, both which had a spoiler and mags.
April 21, 2003	(8:03 pm) Max launches 'CyberScrub' on his computer, at his parents' home at Trouts Road, Stafford.
April 22, 2003	(10:03 am) Max makes a four-second phone call from his mobile to Archana's work phone. Police allege this is to check if she is at work, and answering her phone, and ensure the coast is clear for him to return to the house.

April 22, 2003	(1:56 pm) Max allegedly arrives at the Singhs' home to invite them to watch a movie with him and his two children. He later tells police he searched downstairs before following the family dog, Bujo, upstairs. However, painters working on a neighbouring house say they saw him pass the dog out to his two children in the backyard.
April 22, 2003	(2:30 pm) Max rings his parents and tells them 'Neelma's dead.'
April 22, 2003	(2:33 pm) Max makes a call to 000 but is disconnected.
April 22, 2003	(2:34 pm) Emergency service workers call him back. He says, 'I've got three dead bodies in a bathtub.'
April 22, 2003	(2:38 pm) Max's parents, Carlo and Anna Maria, arrive at Grass Tree Close.
April 22, 2003	(2:49 pm) The first police officers arrive at the home. Neelma, Kunal and Sidhi are soon found deceased by police.
April 22, 2003	(2:59 pm) The Grass Tree Close home is declared a crime scene and a forensic investigation begins.
April 22, 2003	(4:57 pm) Detectives interview Max at Petrie Police Station, with Max's father, Carlo, also in attendance. A Major Incident Room is set up at the Petrie Criminal Investigation (CIB) branch. The investigation is assigned the operational name of Operation Bravo-Settler.
April 22, 2003	(5 pm AEST)—Shirley receives a phone call in Fiji (7 pm local time), the caller telling her that her children have been shot.

April 22, 2003	(9:35 pm) During a search of Max's parents' house at Trouts Road police identify 'CyberScrub' running on the home computer.
April 22, 2003	Max is formally interviewed by police.
April 23, 2003	Vijay and Shirley return to Brisbane from Fiji via Sydney.
April 25, 2003	(9:30 am) Max sobs as he conducts a 'walk-through' of the Singh family home, retracing his footsteps.
April 25, 2003	Max is formally interviewed by police again.
April 25, 2003	A Major Incident Room is established at Petrie Police Station.
April 26, 2003	Vijay and Shirley visit the John Tonge Centre, the mortuary for Queensland Health Forensic and Scientific Services in Coopers Plains, to identify the bodies of their three children.
April 26, 2003	Vijay and Shirley are formally interviewed by police.
April 27, 2003	Shirley's 52nd birthday—her first without her children.
April 29, 2003	Vijay and Shirley return to their Bridgeman Downs house for the first time since the murders.
May 5, 2003	The murder weapon, the garden fork from the Singh garage, is found by police.
May 13, 2003	Police allow Vijay and Shirley to return to their Bridgeman Downs home to stay, in preparation for the childrens' funeral.
May 14, 2003	The funeral is held for Neelma, Kunal, and Sidhi. Max is evicted by police from the service after Singh family members advise police that he is not welcome.

May 17, 2003	Max claims he is being targeted by police and hunted by the media. He says he was in an 18-month relationship with Neelma and wanted to marry her but was opposed by her father.
May 22, 2003	The Singh family denies Max was formally dating their daughter at the time of her death.
July 13, 2003	Brisbane's main metropolitan newspaper, *The Courier-Mail*, writes of Max's 'frustrated desire' to be a police officer. According to a report tendered by psychologist Tony Robinson during sentencing for 83 offences in 1993, Max had the ambition from an early age.
October 2003	Andrea Bowman advises Joe Zitny she is in contact with Max regarding the murders.
August 4, 2003	Kunal's 19th birthday. Shirley attempts to take her life. She stays 13 nights at the Prince Charles Hospital Mental Health Unit.
December 2003	Shirley ends up in the mental health unit again.
February 18, 2004	Shirley is transported to the mental health unit again after downing wine and Stilnox and phoning for the police commissioner. She tells responders she will set fire to her house.
February 26, 2004	Shirley is discharged from hospital.
March 7, 2004	Shirley ends up in the mental health unit again. She is labelled as 'depressed, fidgety and judgement-impaired.'
March 26, 2004	At the request of the police, Andrea Bowman records a conversation with Max.
March 31 to April 1, 2004	Max is formally interviewed by police. The interview starts at 1:30 pm on March 31 and ends at dawn the next morning.

April 6, 2004	Police execute search warrants at Max's sisters' homes in Enoggera and Everton Hills. They remove items including clothing.
April 21, 2004	At the request of police, Andrea Bowman records another conversation with Max.
November 11, 2004	Vijay provides his witness statement to Queensland Police.
October 2005	According to R v Sica 2012 (QSC 5), the police become increasingly concerned for Andrea Bowman's safety and stop asking her to tell them of her discussions with Max. Andrea continues to communicate with Max.
April 2006	Andrea Bowman and Max discuss by phone 'various scenarios' to explain how the murders could have happened.
December 17, 2006	State Coroner Michael Barnes predicts an arrest or inquiry into the children's murders, saying it is time to bite the bullet. Police say they are still making progress.
May 6, 2007	Detective Senior Sergeant Bryan Paton retires from the case, citing health problems.
March 16, 2008	Max told Andrea Bowman it was difficult to strangle someone when they said 'please don't, don't please.'
July 25, 2008	Police again question builders who worked on the Singh house and take DNA samples. The builders are cleared and the case is termed as still active as evidence mounts.
December 20, 2008	Police eliminate the last two DNA profiles found in the Singh home.
December 22, 2008	Max marries his girlfriend, Shivanjani 'Shiv' Arti Kumar.

December 30, 2008	(5:24 am) At his Bribie Island home, Max is arrested for the murders of Neelma, Kunal, and Sidhi.
December 30, 2008	(10:20 am) Max is formally charged.
January 2, 2009	The bail hearing for Max is adjourned. Justice Jim Douglas tells Michael Byrne (QC for Max) that his client's criminal history showed 'a man with serious problems with the law and how to behave in society.'
January 27, 2009	Max is refused bail on fears he could flee.
August 13, 2009	The committal hearing starts. It will run for 95 days over the course of the next 18 months.
December 2009	Max makes a second bid for bail, which is refused despite his father offering a $900,000 surety. He later loses an appeal against this bail refusal.
December 2010	Max is committed to stand trial for murder.
August 2011	Max loses a bid for a judge only trial.
January 31, 2012	Max pleads Not Guilty to three charges of murder on the first day of his trial. It takes prosecutors more than an hour to read the list of 843 possible witnesses. The trial is adjourned until February 13.
June 27, 2012	The jury retires at 10:11 am to consider its verdict on the 76th day of the trial. Deliberations begin after they hear almost four months of evidence.
July 3, 2012	The jury finds Max guilty of murdering Neelma, Kunal, and Sidhi.
July 5, 2012	Max is sentenced to 35 years for murdering Neelma, Kunal, and Sidhi.
July 27, 2012	Max files an appeal against his sentences.

September 2, 2013	Max's appeal against his murder charges is dismissed.
April 11, 2019	Lawyer Jeff Johnson, working for free for Max, claims he has substantial fresh evidence based on forensic drowning research published in 2017. A petition for a pardon is handed to Queensland Governor Paul de Jersey.
January 2020	Max accuses the Queensland Governor and Attorney-General of meddling in his bid to overturn his convictions.
February 4, 2020	Archana dies, aged 43, of a brain aneurysm in Victoria.
May 7, 2020	Archana's funeral is held.
March 9, 2021	Bujo (the family dog present during the murders) dies.
August 2021	Max alleges the Attorney-General Shannon Fentiman did not act in good faith when considering his petition to have her refer his case back to the appeal court.
September 2021	Queensland Government introduces what it calls the 'toughest parole laws in the nation' for prisoners serving life sentences for 'heinous crimes.' The legislation is included in the *Police Powers and Responsibilities and Other Legislation Amendment Bill 2021*.[53]
November 26, 2021	Max loses a court bid to overturn the Attorney-General's decision and is ordered to pay the Attorney General's costs.

April 27, 2022	As Police Assistant Commissioner Mike Condon prepares for retirement, he names the Singh case as the one that stands out most in his mind. The case occurred less than a year after Mr Condon took leadership of the Homicide Squad.

ENDNOTES

[1] Murray, D. (2020, February 5). *Max Sica: the making of a psychopath.* The Courier-Mail.

[2] Ibid.

[3] Campbell, J.R. (1951). Pacific Islands Development Program. *Dealing with disaster: hurricane response in Fiji.*

[4] Best Fiji Guide. (2014). *Fiji Provinces, Districts and Villages.*

[5] National Library of New Zealand. *Arrival of the coolie ship Leonidas, from Calcutta, at Levuka.* Retrieved August 11, 2022.

[6] Girmit.org. Retrieved October 24, 2022.

[7] Britannica. *History of Fiji.* Retrieved February 14, 2022.

[8] Lamb, D. (1987, June 20). *Fiji Coup on Race Issue Means a Paradise Lost.* Los Angeles Times.

[9] Nanda, Ved P. (1992) *Ethnic Conflict in Fiji and International Human Rights Law,* Cornell International Law Journal: Vol. 25: Iss. 3, Article 5.

[10] Kristof, N. (1987, May 21). *Scores of Indians Are Injured as Riots Sweep Fiji.* The New York Times.

[11] Alley, R. (1987). *The military coup in Fiji,* The Round Table, 76:304, 489-496, DOI: 10.1080/00358538708453840

[12] Oberhardt, M. (2012, April 12). *Sica saw blood at house.* The Courier-Mail.

[13] Oberhardt, M. (2012, April 16). *Max Sica murder trial hears accused killer told police God was responsible for the murders of Singh siblings in Brisbane.* The Courier-Mail.

[14] R v Sica (2012) QSC 429. Retrieved November 1, 2022.

[15] Queensland Government (13 August 2022). *Queensland WWII Historic Places.*

[16] Man jailed over kidnap plot (11 March 2005). *ABC News.*

[17] Brittanica. *Lakshmi.* Retrieved 13 August 2022.

[18] Oberhardt, M. (2012, March 3). *Vijay Singh told wife she had duty to be in threesome, Max Sica trial told.* The Daily Telegraph.

[19] Oberhardt, M. (2012, February 16). *Max Sica called Hindu god on Singh siblings; father, murder trial told.* The Courier-Mail.

[20] Oberhardt, M. (2012, February 29). *Neelma Singh nude photos sent to family and friends as Shirley Singh weeps in court at Max Sica trial.* The Courier-Mail.

[21] Knox, D. (2012, July 25). *Anger over ACA paying for interview in Max Sica case.*

[22] Queensland Courts Coroners Court of Queensland Findings of Inquest (2019). 2009/1210 (Inquest into the disappearance and death of Daniel James Morcombe).

[23] Bean, J. (2021, January 8). *Bodies in the Barrels; the Snowtown murders.* Medium.

[24] Brennan, R. (2013, February 22). *Listening devices in Max Sica's house found no evidence of child sex abuse, trial hears.* The Courier-Mail.

[25] R v Sica (2013) QDC 39.

[26] Sica v DPP QLD (2010) QCA 18.

[27] R v Sica (2012) QSC 429.

[28] Fiji Sun (2012, March 16). Retrieved November 1, 2022. *Sica tells of kidnap plot.*

[29] R v Sica (2012) QSC 5.

[30] Oberhardt, M. (2012, May 24). *Singh murders: Max Sica's friend Andrea Bowman say she was 'like a yo-yo' over whether he was a killer.* The Courier-Mail.

[31] Ibid.

[32] Ibid.

[33] Singh, H. (2012). *Evidential Value of Footprints in Criminal Investigation.* ResearchGate.

[34] Oberhardt, M. (2012, April 30). *Footprint left at Singh family murder scene could belong to Max Sica, court told.* The Courier-Mail.

[35] R v Sica (2013) QCA 247.

[36] Fiji Sun (2012, May 17). Retrieved November 1, 2022. *Sock imprint at Singh home 'not conclusive'.*

[37] Oberhardt, M. (2012, July 3). *Sica found guilty of Singh Murders.* Herald Sun.

[38] AAP (2012, August 2). *Sica didn't murder Singh siblings: brother.* News.com.au.

[39] R v Sica (2013). QCA 247.

40 Carson, V and Dibben, K. (2021, January 16). *Max Sica accuses Governor of meddling in his bid for pardon*. The Courier-Mail.

41 Sica v Attorney-General for the State of Queensland (2021) QSC 309.

42 myPolice Queensland Police News (2013, August 12). *Medal Ceremony honours dedicated service.*

43 Kyriacou, K. (2013, August 13). *Detectives honoured for tireless work in bringing triple-murderer Max Sica to trial.* Herald Sun.

44 Antrobus, B. (2021, December 6). *Daniel Callum Sica, son of triple murderer Max Sica, jailed for drug trafficking.* News.com.au

45 Chamberlin, T. (2015, November 5). *Max sica's son Daniel mauled by police dog.* Perth Now.

46 Queensland Parole System Review. Retrieved November 1, 2022. *A Review into the Queensland Parole System.*

47 Brice, C. (2016, September 27). *Jill Meagher: Conviction documentary reveals how killer Adrian Bayley was caught.* ABC News.

48 Hobday, L. (2014, December 10). *Greg Anderson inquest: Police shot Luke Batty's father in self-defence, court told.* ABC News.

49 Deutrom, R. (2016, February 9). *Gerard Baden-Clay 'friends' with triple murderer in jail.* The Courier-Mail.

50 Karp, C. (2020, November 23). *Ex-prison guard who watched over Daniel Morcombe's killer reveals how pathetic and hated the notorious paedophile is behind bars.* Daily Mail Australia.

51 Doneman, P. (2020, February 4). *Tragedy as the only surviving Singh sibling dies of brain aneurism in Melbourne.* 7 News.

52 The Queen v Massimo Sica (1993) CA No 239 of 1993.

53 *Police Powers and Responsibilities and other Legislation Amendment Bill 2021.* Retrieved November 2022.

PEPPER PRESS

9 781925 914641